# The Reconciling Community

The Missional Mending of Spiritual and Social
Relationships Through Local Church Ministry

CHARLES H. WARNOCK

Copyright © 2013 Charles H. Warnock. All rights reserved.

Published by Banister River Press, Chatham, Virginia, U. S. A.

No part of this publication, except for brief quotations in reviews and research, may be reproduced or transmitted in any form or by any means, electronic or mechanical, including photocopying, recording, or any information storage or retrieval system, without prior permission in writing from the publisher. For permissions, write to Banister River Press, P. O. Box 344, Chatham, VA 24531-0344, U. S. A.

For additional information about Banister River Press, please visit our website at www.banisterriverpress.com.

All quotations from the Bible, unless otherwise noted, are taken from THE HOLY BIBLE, NEW INTERNATIONAL VERSION®, NIV® Copyright © 1973, 1978, 1984, 2011 by Biblica, Inc.® Used by permission. All rights reserved worldwide.

Library of Congress Catalog Number: 2013917345

**Library of Congress Cataloguing-in-Publication Data**
Warnock, Charles H., 1948-
  The reconciling community : the missional mending of spiritual and social relationships through local church ministry / Charles H. Warnock.
Includes bibliographical references.
ISBN-13: 978-1450502887 (trade pbk. : alk. paper)
ISBN:10-1450502881 (trade pbk. : alk paper)
  1. Warnock, Charles H. 2. Religion / Christian Ministry / Pastoral Resources

# DEDICATION

To Debbie,
whose love for God and others
witnesses to the story of reconciliation
with extraordinary grace and gentleness

## CONTENTS

Acknowledgments

Introduction 3

1 Community Context Past and Present 9

2 Chatham Baptist Church in Memory and Context 25

3 A Review of Select Literature on Reconciliation 40

4 Theology of the Church Reimagined 57

5 Theological and Theoretical Foundations of Reconciliation 73

6 Crafting a Missional Community of Reconciliation 91

7 The Implementation and Evaluation Process 109

Summary and Conclusion 119

Bibliography 125

Endnotes 140

# ACKNOWLEDGMENTS

I am indebted to the members of Chatham Baptist Church for their patience, generosity, concern, and support during my research and writing. I am privileged to be their pastor and I am humbled by their love.

# INTRODUCTION

"A good book," an author once remarked to me, "is both an argument and a story."[1] If I may borrow that description, this book is just that—an argument and a story. At its heart, it is the story of a community of faith called Chatham Baptist Church. Like most stories it begins in a particular place and time: in this case, the antebellum South of 1857. Because of that setting, this is also a story about how sincere Christian faith was corrupted by the unholy alliance of economics and the expedient evil of slavery.

From a wider perspective, it is the story of how the Commonwealth of Virginia, the American South, and the cultural history of the United States influenced the people of God in Chatham, Virginia. Despite their ancestors' belief in the South's "lost cause," members of the church are now striving to be the people of God in the twenty-first century.[2] While this story will look back at the history of events which shaped it, it will also look forward to what the future might hold. God's people have never been perfect, but as churches of Jesus Christ they have been called to the ministry of reconciliation, first with God and then with others.

If that is the story, then the argument of this book is that the story can have a different ending than it has had previously. Those involved in this story today do not have to keep alive the prejudice and discrimination of the past, but they can discover and live out God's call to be a reconciling community. More specifically, this book will present a strategy for congregations, including Chatham Baptist Church, to reimagine themselves as a missional communities of reconciliation. That will take place as congregations learn about reconciliation during worship and small group experiences, and then demonstrate the practice of reconciliation through church-initiated community reconciliation projects. To do so, each congregation will have to face its history with honesty and clarity, repent of past failures, and craft a different future. If that happens, the generations to come will have a new legacy of Christian witness on which to build.

The argument without the story would be just another exercise in abstract academic thinking. The story without the argument would be a walk down the memory lane of history, clouded by self-deception. Together the story and the argument will create a space for the congregation of Chatham Baptist Church, and other churches, to dream a new dream for church and for community—a dream of reconciliation that heals the wounds of the past and creates faith for the future.

Over fifty years ago, a renown Baptist minister stood before a sea of hopeful people in the shadow of the Lincoln Memorial to share the dream God had given him. On that day the Rev. Dr. Martin Luther King, Jr. said, "I have a dream that one day on the red hills of Georgia, sons of former slaves and sons of former slave-owners will be able to sit down together at the table of brotherhood."[3]

Regrettably, Dr. King's dream remains unrealized in many communities across America. Alienation and inequality have not diminished with the gains of the civil rights movement, but are more prevalent in American society today than even forty years ago.[4] Black and White, rich and poor, educated and unskilled—these represent some of the groups at odds in today's American communities, including my own community of Chatham, Virginia.

In the town of Chatham, standing as silent witnesses to their Christian faith, seven churches raise their steeples to the sky. Four are White churches, and three are African-American congregations. In surrounding Pittsylvania County and the city of Danville, a similar assortment of single-race congregations dots the landscape. In this community, Sunday at eleven o'clock is still "the most segregated hour" of the week.[5] While White and Black churches have held joint worship services on special occasions, those services neither have built lasting bonds between congregations nor healed the hurts of our shared history.

Martin Luther King, Jr. recognized that churches have a role to play in tearing down barriers and in building bridges to that vision he called "the beloved community."[6] "The end is reconciliation, the end is redemption, the end is the creation of the beloved community," according to King. In the beloved community, persons and groups are reconciled to one another by God's "divine love in lived social relation."[7]

The Apostle Paul affirmed the Church's mission as one of reconciliation. "All this is from God, who reconciled us to himself through Christ and gave us the ministry of reconciliation" (2 Corinthians 5:18).[8] While many churches understand reconciliation primarily as a "private affair between God and the individual,"[9] less emphasis has been placed on reconciliation between persons and groups within local communities.[10] This book will address that lack of balance in the ministry of reconciliation, and will offer a roadmap for local churches to become reconciling communities within their ministry contexts.

In the history of Chatham Baptist Church, and its community and state, the type of reconciliation still needed is racial reconciliation. However, although this book will use racial reconciliation for example and discussion, other types of reconciliation will also be explored.

Reconciliation, according to the *Ubuntu* theology[11] of Archbishop Desmond Tutu, is "bringing together that which is separated, alienated ruptured, sick, or broken."[12] Reconciliation, Tutu argues, is the ministry of the Church and the "center of our life and work as Christians."[13] In a community like Chatham, there is much that needs to be reconciled. Virginia's history boasts both the grand and glorious, as well as the dark and ignominious. From the colonial era through the Civil War, Virginia's slave trade was robust. "Life, liberty, and the pursuit of happiness"—words penned by Virginian Thomas Jefferson—did not apply to Africans brought in chains involuntarily to the South.[14] The lingering effects of slavery, and the living descendants of slaves and slave-owners, make it impossible for those in the Chatham area to escape the injustices of the past.

Reconciliation has also been defined as "a journey from the past into the future, a journey from estrangement to communion, or from what was patently unjust in search of a future that is just."[15] Given Virginia's colonial history, its role in the Civil War, and its resistance to desegregation, reconciliation must revisit the past with honesty, and then forge a new way forward. In order to provide a model for the local church as a reconciling community, the congregation of Chatham Baptist Church in Chatham, Virginia will be the locus for this study.

Chatham Baptist Church's unique history makes it an appropriate advocate for a ministry of reconciliation. Located in the county seat of only twelve hundred residents, the church is surrounded by charming nineteenth century homes on tree-lined streets. But the effects of racial tensions, mill town paternalism, and economic downturn have fostered alienation among various groups. Moreover, the church often has accommodated this alienation, rather than challenging it.

Despite that, the church has had a constructive influence in its 155-year history by creating four significant community institutions. With an aging membership, this 175-member congregation must learn from its past and reinvent itself for the future. While limited attempts have been made to address social divisions, Chatham's residents need intentional opportunities for reconciliation. To meet the challenges of church and community, this book presents a strategy for Chatham Baptist Church, and others, to reimagine churches as missional communities of reconciliation, transforming relationships within their geographic context.[16]

The goal of this book is to reimagine the church as a missional community of reconciliation by learning about and engaging in reconciling practices. To craft a ministry not captive to popular self-help clichés, reconciliation must be understood in its multi-faceted expression across disciplines. A pilot project will ground the ministry model theologically while surveying the literature on reconciliation, the missional church, and ecclesiology, so that the congregation's practice can be informed and intentional.

Chapters One and Two concern the ministry context of community and church. Attention to the lingering impact of racial tension and social inequity will show how they contribute to polarization. Current demographic research will note the significance of race, education, and economics. An examination of the church's history will highlight its negative and positive impact. Finally, a look at recent projects the church has initiated toward community reconciliation will help point the way forward.

Chapter Three will survey the academic literature representative of the multiple disciplines and approaches in reconciliation studies. Chapters Four and Five will explore the theological and theoretical foundations of ecclesiology and reconciliation. An alternative ecclesiology will be proposed after examining and critiquing historic Southern Baptist church characteristics. The desired future will be an ecclesiology influenced by the importance of individuality-in-community in Anabaptist theology. Reconciliation will be surveyed in theology, forgiveness studies, peace building, conflict resolution, and restorative justice with an emphasis on the primacy of theology.

In order to guide the church toward re-imagining its ministry, an eight-week pilot project is described in Chapter Six. Detailed attention will be given to the pilot project's goals, participants, leadership, content, and evaluation. Members will learn about reconciliation across disciplines, examine the church's ministry, dialogue with the community, design a community reconciliation project, and evaluate the results. The pilot project will provide a model for a future church-wide event, which is discussed in Chapter Seven. Finally, the Summary and Conclusion wraps up the thesis of the book and indicates a wider application of principles explored here for North American evangelicals and mainline churches.

My passion for this project stems from a desire to foster reconciliation within the church and community where I serve as pastor. In December 2005, our small, historic White congregation opened its doors to host a Boys and Girls Club, the first afterschool club in our county. As a result of that decision dozens of children, Black and White, descended on the church fellowship hall each weekday afternoon. This was the church's first experience hosting a racially-integrated program.

## THE RECONCILING COMMUNITY

Because of the church's involvement with the Boys and Girls Club, Chatham Baptist Church was asked to host the 2007 Martin Luther King Day celebration in Chatham. At the conclusion of the program that day, the African-American pastor presiding asked everyone in the congregation to stand, join hands, and sing "We Shall Overcome." Before we began to sing, he looked at me as I stood at the front of the sanctuary. He said, "Pastor, people notice what you're doing here." His words of encouragement confirmed what I had hoped for--reconciliation was possible in our community.

Some might argue that the alienation brought about by slavery, Jim Crow laws, and segregation is a forgotten chapter in a long dead past. Douglas Massey, however, argues against that notion in his book, *Categorically Unequal*:

> History aside, there are also good social scientific reasons to expect that categorical mechanisms of racial stratification will prove resistant to change. We know, for example, that once learned, cognitive structures do not simply disappear. Racial schemas honed over generations tend to persist in the minds of adults and get passed on to children in conscious and unconscious ways.[17]

The story that is passed on to the children of any community is important. In the past children of Chatham, Danville, and Pittsylvania County were bequeathed a legacy of prejudice and discrimination. This book reflects the desire of the members of Chatham Baptist Church to imagine and live out a new legacy through a ministry of reconciliation. That would be a new story for this community, and one worth passing on to future generations.

# CHAPTER 1

# COMMUNITY CONTEXT PAST AND PRESENT

In order to understand the role Chatham Baptist Church has played in its community in the past, and how it might develop a ministry of reconciliation in the future, it will be helpful to look at the context in which the church is situated. This chapter will examine the historical, economic, sociological, and theological forces that have shaped the region, including the town of Chatham, Pittsylvania County, and the city of Danville. The influence of the Commonwealth of Virginia, the South as a region, and the United States also will be featured where each has contributed to the ethos of the church's community.

## A Picturesque Community and Its Past

Chatham Baptist Church is located a block west of Main Street in downtown Chatham, the county seat of Pittsylvania County. The official website identifies Chatham as "the prettiest little town in Southside Virginia." Eighteenth and nineteenth century homes line Main Street, and there are other buildings of historic interest such as the 1857 Courthouse, the 1813 clerk's office, and the recently restored Chatham train depot. These historic structures along Chatham's tree-lined streets provide a picturesque setting for residents and visitors to the region.[18]

## THE RECONCILING COMMUNITY

Founded in 1777 during the American Revolution, Pittsylvania County drew its name from an English politician, "The Great Commoner," William Pitt. Pitt, later the first Earl of Chatham, was former prime minister of England, and a defender of the American colonies. Pitt insisted that the American colonists should be supported "on English grounds because they were ourselves (sic) put down somewhere else."[19] Eventually in 1852, the name of the county seat of Pittsylvania County was changed to its present name of Chatham, reflecting the continuing admiration for Pitt that had developed during the American colonial era.[20]

That information may seem quaint and irrelevant to the task at hand, but the history of the area's past holds the key to understanding it today. The community celebrates its historic roots through community-wide events such as the "Christmas in Historic Chatham" celebration. The celebration takes place on the first Friday night in December each year, when the citizens of the town gather in front of the antebellum courthouse in the heart of Chatham for an evening of carols by candlelight.[21]

However, since the inception of the Christmas celebration over thirty years ago, scant attention has been given in the community to dialogue regarding the contrast in the historic experiences of the White land owners and their Black slaves, who eventually became their emancipated neighbors and fellow-citizens. While today's racial relationships in Chatham are cordial, implicit social customs are quietly but carefully observed in the community.

Finally, the context of the community cannot be fully appreciated without also including Danville, a city of forty-five thousand residents located seventeen miles south of Chatham and surrounded by Pittsylvania County. Danville was established in 1793 by the tobacco planters of Pittsylvania County as the marketing and transportation hub for their tobacco crop.[22] At the close of the Civil War seventy-two years later, Danville served as the last capitol of the

Confederacy when its President Jefferson Davis fled south from Richmond to escape the Union army.[23] In 1882, the Riverside Cotton Mill was chartered. Eventually Dan River Mills, founded in the 1890s, would become the largest textile producer in the world.[24]

At the height of its textile ascendancy, however, Danville played an infamous role in the American civil rights movement. After a series of demonstrations led by Black ministers beginning on the centennial anniversary of the Emancipation Proclamation, January 1, 1963, Danville descended into a pattern of intimidation toward civil rights demonstrators. The violence reached its height on "Bloody Monday," June 10, 1963, when peaceful marchers were assaulted by Danville police armed with billy clubs and water hoses.[25] When Rev. Dr. Martin Luther King, Jr. visited Danville after "Bloody Monday," he declared, "Very seldom if ever have I heard of a police force being as brutal and vicious as the police have been here in Danville, Virginia."[26]

## Slavery, Tobacco Plantations, and Textile Mills

As Chatham's colonial-themed Christmas celebration and Danville's "Bloody Monday" illustrate, race has played a recurring role in shaping Pittsylvania County, the town of Chatham, and the City of Danville. However, it is tobacco that provides the original connecting thread tying all three jurisdictions together. With land so poor it was unsuitable for other crops, Pittsylvania County became a leading producer of tobacco beginning in the eighteenth century. "In Maryland and Virginia tobacco is our staple, is our all, and indeed leaves no room for anything else," exclaimed Mr. Phillips, a tobacco plantation owner, as quoted in Frederick F. Siegel's book, The Roots of Southern Distinctiveness: Tobacco and Society in Danville, Virginia, 1780-1865.[27]

Siegel describes Virginia's dependence on tobacco as the culprit in the region's developing "Southern backwardness."[28] He cites the following as reasons for that assessment: "the inability to attract a free labor force, the lack of economic diversity, the absence of towns and cities, and the plague of soil exhaustion all antedated the growth of slavery. These problems were directly related to the central fact of Virginia's economic life, the dominance of tobacco."[29] Tobacco, described by historian Larry G. Aaron as a "bewitching vegetable,"[30] became the premier crop of the agricultural economy of Chatham, Pittsylvania County, and ultimately Danville.[31]

Tragically, Virginia also has the regrettable distinction of being the first colony to engage in the American slave trade.[32] In 1619, the first slave cargo of "twenty and odd Negroes"[33] was unloaded at Jamestown, Virginia.[34] However, some of the first slaves to arrive in Virginia are believed to have been Christians, converted in Africa prior to their capture.[35] In addition, the Portuguese slave traders who sold these first slaves were Roman Catholics, and the owners of the slave ships were English Protestants.[36] This contradictory triad of Christianity, economics, and race continued to influence the history of the American South, Virginia, Pittsylvania County, and Chatham for the next four centuries.

Because the cultivation of tobacco required extensive manual labor, slaves were moved quickly from coastal Virginia into Pittsylvania County's burgeoning tobacco plantations. In 1767, the slave population of Pittsylvania County tallied 271. By 1800, 4,200 Africans were held as slaves in the area, more than double the population of White males.[37] By 1860 slave holdings had jumped, with 1,225 slave-holding families owning 14,105 slaves, an average of 12 Black slaves per White household.[38]

Tobacco also influenced the growth of towns and subsequent development of railroads. Along the Dan River, John Wilson operated twenty-eight wagons which transported tobacco and cargo "around the rapids of the Dan River and north to Lynchburg."[39] The city of Danville, rising along the banks of the Dan River, would emerge as the center of tobacco marketing in Southside during the early nineteenth century.[40]

But Danville's story is not just the story of tobacco. In Pittsylvania County and the city of Danville, a convergence of industry and agriculture developed. After the Civil War emancipated slaves in the South, Danville turned to a northern industry—textile manufacturing—to expand the economy. Robert Sidney Smith, in his book, Mill on the Dan: A History of Dan River Mills, 1882-1950, explains that the South's previous "contempt for northern industrial methods gave way to an intense rivalry with those very methods."[41] Textile production grew rapidly and Danville's first textile mill was in operation by 1883.[42] The railroads that transported tobacco out of the region also brought cotton from the plantations of South Carolina into Danville to be woven into fabric at textile mills located adjacent to its tobacco warehouses. Smith writes, "There is no uncertain connection between the prosperity of warehousemen, speculators, and tobacco manufacturers in the 1870's and the town's industrial expansion in the 1880's."[43]

At the close of the Civil War, Danville's population of 7,500 was 60 percent Black. Despite free Blacks being in the majority, Whites demanded preference in the community and at the ballot box. On election day in 1883, Whites who were opposed to Blacks casting ballots started a "race riot" which left four Blacks dead and four wounded. Newspaper accounts shifted the blame for the violence to the city's Black residents. Fearing for their lives, Danville's Black policemen and councilmen resigned, leaving an all-White government and reversing the gains made during Reconstruction.[44]

That same year the first textile mill, Riverside Cotton Mills, began producing goods. When interviewed later, the president of Riverside Cotton Mills, H. R. Fitzgerald, recalled that the mills were established because "there was nothing open for the white working man" and that "race conflicts were constantly brewing."[45] Fitzgerald explained that the cotton mills were started "for the express purpose

## THE RECONCILING COMMUNITY

of affording work to the poor [White] families of the community who were having a hard time."[46]

Unfortunately the racial history of Danville's textile manufacturing is no better than the area's tobacco production. In 1906, Smith records that the mill president reported, "As regards colored people, we only employ them as sweepers, scourers, truck drivers, and in the dye-house and picker-rooms: we do not have them in the mills proper, except in the above-mentioned menial capacities."[47] By 1919, the mill had established a program of "industrial democracy." Mill workers elected representatives to the mill's "House" where mill legislation would be introduced, debated, and voted on by "House" members. One mill "law" which White workers passed read,

> That no colored persons of either sex or any age be employed by our Company inside of Mills in any department or capacity other than sweepers or scourers, or floor cleaners, or janitors except the picker rooms, dyeing and bleachery departments, waste houses, yard force, drivers, truckers, and boiler house. That no colored people can use the same room for dressing or toilet that is used by white people.[48]

By July 1938, Black workers were at the bottom of the pay ladder. Smith writes, "A tally of the payroll for the week ending July 9 showed 423 employees (390 Negro and 33 white) earning less than 30 cents an hour."[49] In 1944, when the mill attempted to employ some Blacks in previously White positions, a backlash resulted in a 30 percent loss of production for the mill. Mill management quickly removed the Black employees from the spinning rooms.[50]

However, the persistent demands by Blacks for the equal protection guaranteed by the Fourteenth Amendment culminated in the civil rights movement of the 1950s and 1960s, which challenged three centuries of racial discrimination in the American South.[51] The landmark Brown v. The Board of Education ruling by the Supreme

Court in 1954 struck down the "separate-but-equal" educational system favored by communities in the South. In addition to the Kansas case, a Virginia case, Davis v. County School Board of Prince Edward County, was included in the Supreme Court ruling.[52]

A year after Brown, the Supreme Court of the United States issued an implementation order mandating school desegregation for the state of Virginia. Invoking a campaign of statewide "massive resistance" led by United States Senator Harry Byrd, Virginia's governor padlocked its public schools in 1958, rather than allowing them to be integrated.[53] In Prince Edward County, east of Pittsylvania County, public schools remained closed from 1958 through 1964, until federal courts forced them to re-open.[54] Even landmark legislation such as The Civil Rights Act of 1964, which provided Blacks with access to public accommodations, could not guarantee egalitarian attitudes from the majority White population.

Intentional racial insensitivity still exists in Virginia more than forty years after the passage of civil rights legislation. In 2010, Virginia's Governor Bob McDonnell reversed the practice of two previous governors by declaring April "Confederate History Month." McDonnell, who is White and holds degrees from the evangelical Regent University, made no mention of slavery as a factor in the Civil War in his proclamation.[55] Instead McDonnell reframed the Civil War as a struggle for Southern independence.[56]

Sheila Johnson, an African-American who co-founded Black Entertainment Television, previously had supported McDonnell. However in a public statement of rebuke Johnson broke with McDonnell, issuing a critique of McDonnell's proclamation:

> I must condemn Governor McDonnell's Proclamation honoring "Confederate History Month," and its insensitive disregard of Virginia's complicated and painful history, the remnants of which many Virginians still wrestle with today. The complete omission of slavery from an official government document,

which purports to be a call for Virginians to "understand" and "study" their history, is both academically flawed and personally offensive. If Virginians are to celebrate their "shared history," as this proclamation suggests, then the whole truth of this history must be recognized and not evaded.[57]

Days later McDonnell apologized and amended his proclamation to include a paragraph lamenting the history of slavery in Virginia.[58]

Another local story illustrates the racial divide that still exists in small Virginia communities like Chatham. In December 2005, after Chatham Baptist Church agreed to host a new unit of the Boys and Girls Club in its building, only one child enrolled during the first week of registration. Because the opening of the new Boys and Girls Club had been widely publicized in Chatham, racial issues appeared to play an invisible role. As pastor of the church, I called one of the African-American pastors in the community, Rev. Otelia Barksdale, pastor of the New Hope A. M. E. Church, which is located two blocks from Chatham Baptist Church.

I asked Rev. Barksdale why Black children were not enrolling, and she explained, "In Chatham, there are 'us' things and 'them' things." Her implication was clear. There existed an unspoken agreement that Black Chatham residents did not attend White events. I asked in reply, "Would you help get the word out that the Boys and Girls Club is 'our' thing?" She agreed. During the next two weeks over fifty children, Black and White, were enrolled. Membership eventually soared to over two hundred children, with approximately sixty children attending each day. Even though implicit racial segregation still exists in Chatham, the Boys and Girls Club experience served as an encouraging sign that reconciliation might be possible.

### A Community Characterized by Diversity and Division

The 2010 United States Census data provides a statistical profile of Pittsylvania County, the town of Chatham, and the adjacent city of Danville. Those census figures demonstrate that the region's population is primarily White and Black, and is divided by educational and economic factors. As will be apparent, the region fares poorly in population growth, educational attainment, and economic prosperity compared both to the Commonwealth of Virginia and to the United States population as a whole.[59] However, there are some indicators of hope, and in some categories the downward slide has been either stopped or reversed.

The 2010 population of the region has decreased by 3 percent since the 2000 U. S. Census. Population changes from the 2000 to the 2010 census break down as follows: Pittsylvania County increased 3 percent from 61,745 to 63,506; Danville decreased 11 percent from 48,411 to 43,055; and the town of Chatham decreased 5 percent from 1,338 to 1,269. Compared to Virginia's 13 percent increase statewide, the area's decline puts it 16 percent behind the state growth average for 2000 to 2010.[60]

The population figures also provide an analysis of the area's population by race. In Danville, Whites decreased to 47 percent, while Blacks increased to 48 percent of the total population, becoming the city's new majority. In Pittsylvania County, Whites increased by half a percent to 75.5 percent of the county population, compared to Blacks who decreased slightly to 22 percent of the county's total. Chatham's White population increased to 73 percent of the town's residents, compared to Blacks' decrease of almost 3 percent to 23 percent of the town's total. Across Virginia, the average state population racial profile is now 68.6 percent Whites, and 19.4 percent Blacks, with other racial groups making up the balance of the state population. In other words, Whites and Blacks both claim a higher percentage in Chatham and the county than in the state; also, the Black population of Danville is almost three times the percentage of the state average.[61]

Despite the area's population decline, the educational attainment data in both Danville and Pittsylvania County provides some reason for hope.[62] Educational attainment, a key community benchmark, improved overall in both the county and city of Danville, but both still lag behind Virginia's state averages.[63] In Danville city schools, the high school graduation rate increased from 68.5 percent in 2000 to 76 percent in 2009. Pittsylvania County posted almost identical numbers rising from 67.3 percent to 76.6 percent for the same period. However, while this rate is a significant improvement, high school graduation still falls roughly 10 percent behind the Virginia state average.[64]

## A Community Struggling to Win the Future

By the last decade of the twentieth century, the die was cast for the demise of the region's economic engines. A report from a community group called Jobs for the Future cites, "Since 1990, the Danville region has lost over 15,000 jobs. Many of the Danville region's core industrial employers . . . have either gone out of business or sought economies with lower pay scales on other shores, leaving in their wake thousands of laid off local, low-skilled manufacturing workers."[65] The decline of these industries created soaring unemployment in the Danville region long before the nationwide 2008 recession. A former Dan River employee voices the dilemma of laid-off, low-skill workers:

> My grandmother, my mother, and my two sisters all worked at the mill (Dan River). My mother got me a part-time job at the mill (Dan River) the summer of the eleventh grade. When the summer was over, I had gotten used to having some money in my pocket and being able to buy nice clothes, so I left school and went to work full-time. . . . I worked in maintenance for 20 years until the plant closed two years ago. . . . The mill was a good job. I was making twelve dollars an hour. I know that doesn't sound like much, but with the over-time and the double-

time on weekends, I was able to keep my car and buy my own house. I didn't have to worry about nothing except getting to work. . . . Since I was laid off, I have been getting Trade Act money and I am studying to get my GED. When I'm finished I hope to get a job in retail or food service.[66]

While the economic impact is significant in itself, the increasing divide between the employed and unemployed, the affluent and poor, also tears at the social fabric of a community. A recent poll released by the Pew Research Center showed that 66 percent of all respondents believed that there were "very strong" or "strong" conflicts between rich and poor.[67] When separated by race, 74 percent of Blacks and 65 percent of Whites surveyed thought that conflicts existed between rich and poor. While the Black percentages increased 8 percent from a similar survey in 2009, the White respondents who saw conflict between economic classes increased by 22 percent since the same survey two years before.

Interestingly, only 38 percent of total respondents said that conflicts existed between Blacks and Whites. This response might indicate that economic class is now the new euphemism for race when expressing societal conflict. Sherrow Pinder thinks so. In her book, Whiteness and Racialized Ethnic Groups in the United States, she writes, "Very often culture is substituted for race, or class is substituted for race. When the latter happens, it does so because America's class system is distinctively racialized."[68]

Leaving the issue of race and class for a moment, the solution to unemployment due to plant closings is attracting new industry to the region. However, the skills needed for textile work and tobacco farming are not the same skills needed to work in the high technology industries the region hopes to attract.[69] The challenge of raising worker skill and education levels to attract new employers is being tackled by educational institutions like Galileo Magnet High School which opened in 2002; the Institute for Advanced Learning and Research, which opened in 2004; the Regional Center for Advanced Technology & Training which opened in 2005; and Danville Community College. The Danville Regional Foundation monitors academic attainment as one of its benchmark goals.[70]

Despite educational achievements, a broader civic dialogue is needed to engage more segments of the population as future leaders in the region. The Jobs for the Future report observes, "Another legacy of mill town culture and its isolated, low-skilled workers is a lack of community-based institutional and leadership capacity, particularly within the region's African American community."[71] For many, however, the pathway to community leadership remains blocked. One aspiring community leader remarked,

> There are some key organizations in our community that, at least according to perception, are closed. For the most part they are comprised of "Good Old Boys" and the people who are acceptable to them. . . . No one under age 30 and they are mostly male. What's strange is that these groups pride themselves on being a visionary reflection of the needs of the community, yet they have few women, only token minorities, and no one under the age of 30.[72]

Despite the roadblocks thrown up to new leaders by established organizations, the region has turned again to institutions to reinvent itself. Two institutions have set the tone for the revitalization of the Danville-Pittsylvania County region. First, The Institute for Advanced Learning and Research was built as a joint effort by both Pittsylvania County and the City of Danville, and funded by Virginia's Tobacco Indemnification and Community Revitalization Commission.[73] The Institute is a satellite campus of Virginia Tech, but also offers both undergraduate and graduate degrees through affiliated educational institutions. However the primary purpose of The Institute is to conduct state-of-the-art research into four areas: horticulture and forestry, motorsports and vehicle performance, renewable energy and bio-products, and robotics systems. By building on the agricultural and manufacturing history of the region, The Institute "develops and attracts technology and talent to serve as a catalyst for economic and community transformation for Southern Virginia."[74]

The second institution that is shaping the redevelopment of the Danville-Pittsylvania County region is The Danville Regional Foundation. The Foundation's mission is displayed on its website:

> The Danville Regional Foundation is a catalyst for innovation and an agent for transformation. Understanding that significant community change takes time, the Foundation invests for the long term in efforts that promise sustained positive impact for the Dan River region. The Foundation is committed to development, promotion, and support of activities, programs, and organizations that address the health, education, and well-being of the region's residents.[75]

The Foundation was established with funds from the sale of the community-owned hospital, Danville Regional Medical Center. The sale resulted in a $200 million windfall which became the asset base of a community charitable trust. Each year the Foundation expends approximately 5 percent of its endowment to fund local charities, to commission studies of the community, and to stimulate growth and private development.

## A Community United and Divided by Faith

These new institutions are welcomed additions to the community, but one institution has endured through all of the region's epochal changes from the eighteenth into the twenty-first centuries. That institution is the local church. Collectively churches in this community have served as repositories of memory, keepers of tradition, and gathering places for individuals and families who share a common faith. The region features the typical complement of civic clubs, social circles, and arts groups, but local churches dominate the social organization landscape.

While Black churches founded after the Civil War became "safe harbors" for freed Blacks, White churches played a much different role.[76] From the historical record it is clear that White churches supported slavery during the Civil War era. Mark Noll, in his book, *The Civil War as a Theological Crisis,* points out that slavery was supported by "Bible believers in the North as well as among Bible believers in the South."[77] During and after the Civil War, Southern churches and preachers continued to justify the South's "lost cause."[78] One hundred years after the Civil War, Rev. Dr. Martin Luther King, Jr. remarked on the absence of Southern White churches in the struggle for the civil rights of African-Americans.[79]

Virginia's lack of racial sensitivity is not due to a lack of Christian churches. In 2010, the state of Virginia had 109 churches per 100,000 residents.[80] However, in Danville the ratio climbs to 133 churches per 100,000 residents;[81] and in the county the figure soars to 202 churches per 100,000 residents.[82] Clearly this is a community of churches. By observation, most of these churches are small congregations served by one professional minister. No evangelical mega-churches exist in the area, and no single church dominates the area's church landscape. The church with the largest combined attendance is Sacred Heart Catholic Church in Danville, the only Roman Catholic church within a twenty-five-mile radius.

Southern Baptists make up the largest single denomination represented in the area. Among forty-six churches affiliated with the Pittsylvania Baptist Association, which includes Chatham Baptist Church, 65 percent reported annual average Sunday worship attendance in 2010 of less than one hundred. Ten churches reported Sunday worship attendance of between one hundred and two hundred, and three had attendance in the low two hundreds. Only two churches recorded higher attendance, and those both averaged in

## THE RECONCILING COMMUNITY

the high four hundreds. Baptists total 24,706 adherents out of 75,561 adherents in all faiths and denominations. In summary, about 25 percent of all churches in the region and about 33 percent of all church adherents are Southern Baptist.[83]

While churches in the area are ubiquitous, Sunday at eleven o'clock in Chatham, Pittsylvania County, and Danville is still the most "segregated hour" of the week.[84] But despite the segregation of congregational life, there are examples of churches initiating outreach across racial barriers. In 2005, as previously noted, Chatham Baptist Church partnered with the Boys and Girls Club of the Danville Area to host the first interracial organization, except public schools, for children and teens in Pittsylvania County. The Chatham club met at the church for three years, moving to the new Community Center at Chatham in June 2008.[85]

Second, the new Community Center at Chatham was the direct result of churches working together across racial lines. Pastors representing the denominational and racial diversity of Chatham and Pittsylvania County were invited to meet at Chatham Baptist Church in August 2005 to discuss the possibility of a new community center for the county. At the time Pittsylvania County did not have any type of recreational facility. The only public recreation facilities in the county then were its schools, and their public use was restricted tightly by the school board.

The meeting of eighteen pastors that day resulted in the formation of a not-for-profit charity, Chatham Cares, which applied for a grant from the Danville Regional Foundation. In July 2006, The Foundation awarded Chatham Cares three million dollars to construct a new community center. The Community Center at Chatham was to host the Boys and Girls Club as its anchor program, and serve as a gathering place for the entire community. The Community Center at Chatham was the first public recreation facility, other than schools, to open to persons of all races in Chatham and

Pittsylvania County.[86]

Chatham Baptist Church also partnered with Virginia Tech and the Renaissance Music Academy of Blacksburg, Virginia to offer music instruction to children. In 2006, instructors in violin, piano, voice, guitar, and cello began giving music lessons to community children on a fee basis. The church was represented on the local steering committee formed to guide the new Chatham Arts Community Music School. Each year about thirty students have enrolled in the program, and a number of students receive partial scholarships based on demonstrated financial need. White and Black students are enrolled in the program, and participation remains steady.[87]

These three programs—the Chatham Boys and Girls Club, The Community Center at Chatham, and Chatham Arts Community Music School—confirm that the community can be brought together across racial barriers. But these attempts have addressed neither the complexities of race relations in the twenty-first century, nor have they fostered dialogue about the racial history of this state and community. Clearly more intentional attempts are needed to bring opportunities for reconciliation to all citizens of the community. However, these three initiatives demonstrate that local churches can bring a diverse community together successfully, and that success creates hope for future reconciliation projects.

## CHAPTER 2

## CHATHAM BAPTIST CHURCH IN MEMORY AND CONTEXT

In the preceding chapter, the community context in which the church is situated was explored from various perspectives. External forces shaping the church's life and ministry include the legacy of slavery, the loss of the region's two primary economic industries, the lingering effects of mill town life, and the failure of White churches to rise above Southern culture. Chatham Baptist Church, like most of its sister churches in this community, accommodated itself to the cultural norms of its day more often than not. However there are areas in which Chatham Baptist Church distinguished itself as a progressive congregation with a commitment to the common good of the community. Those areas offer hope that the church may craft a new chapter in its history, one which draws from a new interpretation of its past, in order to develop a ministry of reconciliation.

The context of life within the congregation of Chatham Baptist Church could be explored from a variety of angles. Churches typically organize their histories into schemes such as pastoral tenure, building programs, significant turning points, or chronology. However, the concern of this book is to highlight those aspects of church history and life that cast light on the church's potential for a ministry of reconciliation.

## A Southern, Small Town Baptist Church

Founded in 1857, Chatham Baptist Church is among the oldest Baptist churches in Pittsylvania County. The church was born in the expansion of the Southern Baptist Convention twelve years after it split from northern Baptists over the issue of slavery.[88] Chatham Baptist Church's history reflects each successive chapter in its community's struggle with racial issues from the antebellum South to the present. From its beginnings, leading figures in local civic life held membership in the congregation. However, "colored servants"—a euphemism for slaves—were also received as members of the church prior to the Civil War, and they "occupied the gallery" during Sunday services.[89]

Chatham Baptist Church also holds the distinction of being the last Baptist church in the area to have a freed slave as a member. According to *The History of Pittsylvania Baptist Association: 1788-1963*, by Chas M. Leek, in 1915, "Aunt Easter, a former slave, was still a member there and regularly occupied a seat at the right end of a center pew about a third of the way down the aisle."[90] The church still occupies the same sanctuary Aunt Easter shared with her White fellow worshippers, an historic 1890 Gothic structure seating 150 on the main floor, and seventy in the gallery.

## Members, Money, and Leaders

Today the most obvious characteristic of Chatham Baptist Church is that it is a small church. Small in this instance means that worship attendance averages about seventy-five persons each Sunday. According to Lyle Schaller, this places the church in the largest cohort of American church attendance—churches averaging between fifty-one and one hundred persons at worship. About 110,000 churches—one in three Protestant congregations in the United States—fall into this category.[91]

Mark Chaves, professor of sociology of religion at Duke University, points out that churches need three things to survive: "members, money, and leaders."[92] Chaves's research also indicates that the median size congregation in the United States has seventy-five persons in attendance.[93] Israel Galindo, in his book, *The Hidden Lives of Congregations: Discerning Church Dynamics,* calls this size "the shepherding-size congregation." By that he means that church members "get their spiritual needs met primarily through their personal relationships with the pastor."[94]

Demographically, the church's membership skews older than the national average. The church has 106 active participants, fifteen years of age or older. The church's age distribution is disproportionately older than the United States worshipping population, except in one category.[95] Chatham Baptist Church also echoes national trends with fewer young adults attending, and with faithful older adults leaving the congregation through death.[96] Church leaders recognize that the church's age profile must be changed if the church is to survive. Table 1 illustrates the age distribution of the church in comparison to the average age of worshippers in the United States, and the age distribution in the general United States population.

**Table 1.** Age Distribution of Chatham Baptist, U. S. Worshippers, and U. S. Population

| Age | Chatham Baptist | U. S. Worshippers | U. S. Population |
| --- | --- | --- | --- |
| 15-24 | 5% | 10% | 18% |
| 25-44 | 20% | 30% | 38% |
| 45-64 | 33% | 36% | 28% |
| 65+ | 42% | 24% | 16% |

**Source:** Chatham Baptist Church percentages from the church's database. Percentages for U. S. worshippers vs. U. S. population from Woolever and Bruce, *A Field Guide to U.S. Congregations*, 13.

The church recognizes the need to reach out to younger prospective members. In a survey of five key church leaders in 2006, all five agreed that the congregation needed "spiritual, numerical, and missional growth."[97] The church is making some progress in the area of numerical growth. In 2010 and 2011, new member additions exceeded membership losses.[98]

While the church is median in membership size in America, its finances are above average. Chatham Baptist is among the 13 percent of all churches nationwide that have "a one-year cushion of monetary savings."[99] To maintain its financial stability in light of an aging membership, the church has decreased its budget each year since 2008. However, even with the budget adjustments, Chatham Baptist Church's annual budget of about $250,000 exceeds the average church budget in median size congregations, which is $56,000.[100] The congregation practices good financial stewardship, has no debt, and monetary resources for ministry and special projects have been available with congregational approval.

To round out Chaves's triad of "members, money, and leaders," he means professional ministers when he uses the term "leaders." In calling its ministers during the past six decades, the church has placed a high value on an educated clergy. Since 1954, the church has called seven pastors, all of whom possessed Master of Divinity degrees. Five of the seven held or earned doctorates during their tenure. The pastor is the only minister on staff, which is typical for forty out of forty-six Baptist churches in this area.[101]

As is the case in most American churches, worship at Chatham Baptist Church is the "primary way" in which the "expression and transmission of religious meaning" is accomplished.[102] In line also with most American churches, more members of Chatham Baptist Church participate in worship than any other single activity.[103] Beyond attending, members also value the experience of worshipping with others and the "feeling of warmness in the smiling faces" gathered each Sunday.[104]

## An Aristocratic Church in Need of a New Vision

In addition to being a small but affluent church, a solo pastorate, and a worshipping congregation, the church has been characterized by some as an "aristocratic" church. With pride older members recall outstanding personalities from the church's past. For instance, the family of John A. T. Robertson was among the church's charter members. As an adult, Robertson became a renowned New Testament scholar and president of Southern Baptist Theological Seminary in Louisville, Kentucky.[105] Other leading members in its

155-year history include a former Virginia Supreme Court justice; local doctors, attorneys, and politicians; and leading community educators and business owners. However, this feeling of exceptionalism can inhibit outreach and inclusiveness. In a personal interview, one member recalled the church in the 1950s when the pews were packed each Sunday. "But," she observed, "the class of people was not as high as it is now."[106]

The "aristocratic" description, however, reveals a looming church problem. Galindo describes one of the later stages in church life cycles as "the aristocracy stage." This stage is a subset of the "maturity stage" and applies to churches with a distinctive heritage. The aristocracy stage is characterized by a church's unique place in its community, an appreciation for traditionalism, clergy professionalism, and "good taste." The aristocratic congregation enjoys a level of influence in its community, and members look back on the church's history with pride.[107] Chatham Baptist Church has the classic marks of this stage in Galindo's church lifespan schema.

The maturity stage, of which the aristocracy stage is a subset, presents unique challenges. Without intervention, churches in the maturity stage will devolve into bureaucratic rigidity in an attempt to control their declining fortunes. The final stage after bureaucracy is dissolution of the church. To recover from the maturity stage, including the aristocracy subset, the church's challenge is to reframe its mission in ways that honor its past, while adopting new ministries for the future.[108]

Alan Roxburgh, in his book, *Missional Map-Making: Skills for Leading in Times of Transition*, calls this task the challenge of "making new maps" which will guide the congregation into a missional future.[109] One example of the church's need to make a "new map" is its conflation of denominational missions programs with the mission of the church. This focus on denominational missions as the church's mission has resulted in the church expending a disproportionate amount of its resources on denominational missions in other countries, rather than on its own mission of ministry in Chatham, Pittsylvania County, and Danville.

# THE RECONCILING COMMUNITY

## Lay Leadership and Church Decision-making

While new directions are needed, the work and administration of the church will most likely remain consistent with that of other traditional Southern Baptist congregations.[110] According to the church's constitution and by-laws, decision-making is vested in the congregation through "democratic business meetings."[111] Member-led committees are a key component of the congregation's administration. These cover areas such as finance, personnel, building and grounds, food services, music, ordinances, altar flowers, library, nursery, social gatherings, and transportation. In addition, program directors, missions leaders, and Sunday school teachers are also elected annually.[112] Finally, the elected Board of Deacons, consisting of men and women, gives oversight to the church in cooperation with the pastor.[113]

Fifty-seven of the church's 106 active adult members serve in some elected capacity. Chatham Baptist Church exceeds the national average of 38 percent member participation, involving 54 percent of its members in some type of leadership role.[114] Others, while not serving in elected positions, are voluntary members of small groups such as the adult choir, adult Sunday school classes, or adult women's mission and Bible study groups.

In addition to member involvement, the church has taken progressive social positions over the past forty years, despite the region's conservative political environment.[115] These include gender inclusivity, reflected in electing women as deacons and administrative leaders; fostering local ecumenical cooperation; and supporting higher education, particularly in theologically moderate schools like Baptist Theological Seminary in Richmond. Other moderate Southern Baptist churches also support these progressive positions.[116] This puts the church out of step with the ultra-conservative direction of the Southern Baptist Convention, which began in 1979.[117] However, the church functions with little regard to denominational politics. When asked about the effect of the Southern Baptist rift on the church, one member succinctly said: "That does not concern us much. We are Virginia Baptists!"[118]

Despite its progressive positions and the high level of

member engagement, leaders seem to function without a cohering vision of the church's role in the community. The mission statement in the church's constitution and by-laws is overly broad:

> Chatham Baptist Church is an autonomous, democratic, Bible-based fellowship under the lordship of Jesus Christ. The mission of this church is to be a praying, loving, sharing, caring fellowship of Christians committed to providing worship experiences, Bible study, training in discipleship and church membership, to giving opportunities for service to God and man, and to working with fellow Christians in obedience to the Great Commission, sharing the Gospel with our community and the whole world.[119]

This mission statement touches every base in Baptist ecclesiological practice, but fails to give focus to the life and work of the congregation. A missional church might continue many of the same ministries, but it would do so with focused intentionality.[120] In short, Chatham Baptist Church needs to discern a focused missional ministry in its community, and reconciliation could be the ministry to which the Spirit is leading the church. Craig Van Gelder, in his book, *The Ministry of the Missional Church: A Community Led by the Spirit*, contends, "The Spirit creates a new type of reconciled community through accomplishing redemption and gives this community a new identity as the church of Jesus Christ."[121] Van Gelder further adds, "The Spirit leads these communities [churches] into active ministry."[122]

## A Catalyst for Community Institutions

A close examination of the church's history in establishing community institutions might offer a key to finding a new ministry focus for the church. In the past, Chatham Baptist Church has used its influence in the community to establish four community institutions: Hargrave Military Academy in 1909, Samuel Harris Memorial Baptist Church in 1959, The Chatham Boys and Girls Club in 2005, and The Community Center at Chatham in 2008. The stories behind the founding of each of these institutions can offer helpful guidance as the church seeks to reinvent itself as a missional community of reconciliation.

## Hargrave Military Academy

# THE RECONCILING COMMUNITY

At the beginning of the twentieth century, Virginia Baptists were concerned about the Christian education of their young people. According to Reuben Edward Alley's *A History of Baptists in Virginia*, the Baptist state convention had gone on record in 1889 in support of "more and better academies."[123] Virginia's public education system was successful in larger towns and cities, but it did not function "so well in the rural districts."[124] Concerned for their rural constituency, the Baptist Committee on Education proclaimed, "Let the [Baptist] academy know its place, respect it, fill it fully, while the [Baptist] college crowns its work with a broad and high standard of scholarship."[125] It was in this atmosphere that Virginia Baptists pushed education to the forefront in their state convention.

By the early 1900s, Baptist academies and colleges had been established around the state, but none in Pittsylvania County. However in 1906, Charles R. Warren opened a secular school for boys in Chatham. For three years the Warren Training School struggled financially, finally folding in the summer of 1909.

Hearing that the Warren school had closed, the pastor of Chatham Baptist Church, Rev. T. Ryland Sanford, and two of its most prominent members, Jesse H. Hargrave and his son, J. Hunt Hargrave, seized the opportunity to establish a Baptist school to replace it. Chatham Training School opened in the fall of 1909. The Hargraves, a wealthy banking family in Chatham, quickly purchased land and buildings for the new school. The pastor of Chatham Baptist Church, "young, full of vigor and a great organizer," was installed as its first president.[126] Although church business meeting minutes from that period have been lost, the fact that Rev. Sanford served simultaneously as pastor of the church and as president of Chatham Training School for four years indicates that the congregation supported the new institution and the church's involvement with it. In 1925 the school's name was changed to Hargrave Military Academy "as a permanent memorial to J. Hunt Hargrave."[127]

In the first sixty years of its existence, Hargrave faculty members were predominantly Baptist, and most were members of Chatham Baptist Church. The majority of cadets also attended Chatham Baptist Church, filling the balcony each week. This practice ended in early 1970 when Hargrave completed a chapel on its campus and began conducting Sunday services there. Although the ties to faculty and cadets are less obvious now than in the past, Chatham Baptist Church maintains a cooperative relationship with Hargrave Military Academy.

Hargrave Military Academy has also influenced social life in Chatham. While local Baptist churches lagged behind in race relations, Hargrave Military Academy led the community in bridging racial barriers. Black cadets were admitted to Hargrave in 1971, when "the Board of Trustees passed a resolution that Hargrave would not consider race, color, or country of origin in its admission or employment policy."[128]

Today Hargrave Military Academy occupies a 350-acre campus, owns buildings worth $20 million, and enrolls over 250 young men each year. It enjoys an international reputation drawing students from eighteen other countries, including China and Saudi Arabia. The school remains affiliated with Virginia Baptists, and the educational philosophy of providing "an atmosphere on the campus, in the barracks, and in the classroom that is conducive to Christian growth" continues at Hargrave today.[129]

## Samuel Harris Memorial Baptist Church

The second institution the church founded was more typical for Baptist churches in the 1950s. In 1959, Chatham Baptist Church was challenged by the Southern Baptist Convention's "30,000 Movement" to plant a new church.[130] Families in the nearby Fairview community had indicated interest in starting a Baptist church in their community. Although it was only two miles from Chatham Baptist Church, Fairview's working class residents expressed uneasiness at attending Chatham Baptist Church where the community's doctors, lawyers, and community leaders worshipped.

Church planting in the late 1950s was not an easy process, however. The new work had to be sponsored by an existing church in the local association. The sponsoring church was expected to provide members, money, and leaders to the mission until it became a fully functioning Southern Baptist church. Pastoral leadership came from Rev. Eugene Cullum, who assumed the role of mission pastor in addition to pastoring Chatham Baptist Church. Mr. L. R. Clements, a Hargrave teacher, and Col. Aubrey Camden, retired president of Hargrave, led the new mission and constructed its first building.[131] Ten years passed before the congregation had a viable complement of members, money, and leaders and the ability to stand on its own. In 1969, the mission was constituted as Samuel Harris Memorial Baptist Church. In 2010, the church reported seventy-two resident members with an average attendance of forty for Sunday worship.[132]

## The Chatham Boys and Girls Club

In June 2004, I was called as the eighteenth pastor of Chatham Baptist Church. As the church and I sought to chart a different course for the future, it became obvious to me that the community needed a children's afterschool program. In 2004, Pittsylvania County did not own or operate a single recreation facility or park, and had no plans to establish any program of afterschool activities for children. In rural counties children had been expected to work on family farms after school. As tobacco production faded, fewer families farmed, and more children were left alone after school by working parents.

In conversations with others in the community, church leaders discovered that the Danville Boys and Girls Club wanted to open a club in the county. A new club needed a facility that would accommodate fifty students, and provide space for classes and recreation. School buildings would have been a natural solution, but county school board guidelines effectively prohibited their use. In addition to space, funding had to be addressed. The estimated cost of first year operating expenses for a new club in the county was $50,000.

Meetings between church leaders and club representatives, from the fall of 2004 until the summer of 2005, produced little progress in resolving the space and funding issues. Unexpectedly, a grant of $40,000 became available in September 2005, with the stipulation that a new chapter of the Boys and Girls Club had to be operating in the county by the end of 2005. A minimum of one hundred children had to be enrolled, staff hired, and a suitable meeting space reserved by that deadline.

A leading business owner in the community who was chairman of the Board of Deacons at Chatham Baptist Church at the time, supported the desire to establish a Boys and Girls Club in Chatham. He suggested that the church host the new Boys and Girls Club at no cost. Privately he arranged financial support to supplement the Chatham Club through its first year of operation. The deacons of the church approved the proposal. In a church business meeting in October 2005, the congregation voted to host the new club at no charge as the church's contribution to the community. The church also negotiated permission to offer music and art classes to the children of the Chatham Boys and Girls Club.[133]

Beginning in December 2005, the Boys and Girls Club of Chatham met at the church after school each day. Some church members engaged with the children, and the church hosted several dinners and hot dog cookouts for the families of members. Because the church did not have a gym, the church parking lot became the outdoor games area. With the daily presence of sixty Black and White children, the congregation confronted its own feelings about race honestly and constructively. As a result, some Boys and Girls Club members attended church events including Wednesday night suppers and vacation Bible school. In May 2008, after two and a half years of growth at Chatham Baptist Church, sixty members of the Boys and Girls Club marched from the church's building on block south to the new Community Center at Chatham, their new home. The Boys and Girls Club continues to provide opportunities for recreation, learning, and service in a safe environment each weekday after-noon.[134]

## The Community Center at Chatham

Prior to the founding of the Boys and Girls Club, Chatham Baptist Church invited Black and White ministers from the community to a luncheon in August 2005, to discuss the possibility of building a new community center in Chatham. Talks with the Danville Boys and Girls Club had stalled because no suitable facility had been found to house the club. That would change later in the fall, but in August those involved had determined that a new afterschool program required a new building.

The assembled group of eighteen pastors represented an equal number of White and Black churches. The result of that meeting was that the pastors agreed to pursue grant opportunities for a new community center. With the encouragement of church leaders and local pastors, a non-profit organization called Chatham Cares, Inc. (hereafter, Chatham Cares) was formed to own and operate the center. Chatham Cares applied for a grant from the Danville Regional Foundation in January 2006.

Because of Chatham Baptist Church's track record in starting the Boys and Girls Club at the church, Chatham Cares received a grant for $3 million to construct and furnish a new community center in Chatham in July 2006.[135] A business leader and church member gently applied his considerable civic influence as a proponent of the community center, and I served as the first president of Chatham Cares. After two years of planning and construction, the Community Center at Chatham opened to the public in June 2008. Reaction in the community was overwhelmingly positive. For the first time in the area's history, Chatham and Pittsylvania County had a public recreation and meeting facility intentionally created to welcome all community residents, regardless of race. According to plan, the Boys and Girls Club moved from the church to the new community center that same month.

In addition to providing a home for the Boys and Girls Club, the community center was designed to be the area's "third place"—a community gathering space like Ray Oldenburg describes in his book, *The Great Gooa Place*. Oldenburg writes, "The first and most important function of third places is that of uniting the neighborhood."[136] To that end the center was designed to appeal to all age groups. The facility contains a full-court gym, a large hall seating 175 people theater-style, an art studio, a media room, a fifteen station computer lab, a large meeting room seating sixty at tables, and a full-service commercial kitchen. The building is equipped with state-of-the-art digital audio and video technology, and wireless Internet connectivity.[137]

The center has succeeded beyond expectation at bringing the community together. When the Boys and Girls Club is not in session, the community center offers classes, rents space for private and business functions, hosts the weekly luncheon of the Chatham Rotary Club, and sponsors a weekly bluegrass concert featuring local musicians. At last count, over ten thousand persons had attended at least one event at the community center in 2011, not including the Boys and Girls Club. The Community Center at Chatham is fulfilling the purpose for which it was constructed: to be a community gathering place for all of the residents of the region. While Chatham Baptist Church does not own the community center, the church's pastor, deacons, and other lay leaders were involved directly in the community center's conception, design, funding, construction, and operation.

All of the institutions that Chatham Baptist Church has facilitated have four factors in common: strong cooperation between pastoral and lay leadership; collaboration with other groups in the community; a concern for the community's welfare; and a commitment to individuals on the margins of society, especially children and youth. The pattern the church has established in conceiving, organizing, and launching these four institutions reflects the church's concern to unite the community. If the church can keep alive its altruistic concern for the community, and build on its past experiences, Chatham Baptist Church can create a ministry of reconciliation in the future.

## Core Ministry Analysis

It would be too simplistic to analyze the church's ministry context as one of merely "members, money, and leaders," although all three have converged at times to create four outstanding community institutions. Beyond that, the evidence points to a church that has exerted its influence over the years to effect positive change that benefitted the community as a whole, not just its members. Chatham does not have a congregation called "First Church," but if it did, there is little doubt that the concern Chatham Baptist Church has exhibited for its community would make it a candidate for that designation.

Baptist churches typically are focused on their own growth and expansion, and Chatham Baptist Church has done that over the years, too. Like most congregations, the church has constructed buildings, raised money, and worked to ensure its continued existence. However, the church also has expended time, energy, and resources to make its community a better place. Hargrave Military Academy has graduated thousands of cadets who have gone on to successful careers in sports, business, medicine, politics, law, and religion. Samuel Harris Memorial Baptist Church, although a small congregation, continues to minister to the spiritual needs of its community effectively. The Chatham Boys and Girls Club offers a safe environment for children after school, and gives children opportunities for learning and service never available before in Chatham or Pittsylvania County. The Community Center at Chatham has become a community gathering place, providing programs and activities that did not exist a few years ago. As a direct result of the success of the community center, the Pittsylvania County Board of Supervisors established a county recreation program and hired its first director in 2010. More important than programs however, the Community Center is a space open to all persons in the community regardless of race, class, or any of the other factors that have divided the community in the past.

The church helped establish these institutions as an expression of its values, and as its contribution to the common good of the community. It has been faithful to its mission to serve the community, cooperate with others, and share the Gospel in many unique ways. The church has exhibited an extraordinary concern for children and young people, and all four institutions it has facilitated focus largely on nurturing children and teens. The church's interest in education is reflected most obviously in its relationship with Hargrave Military Academy, but it is also present in the Christian education programs of the Samuel Harris Church, the social and art education programs at the Community Center, and the life skills courses at the Chatham Boys and Girls Club.

The key to the future of Chatham Baptist Church is to interpret in new ways the narratives that have shaped the congregation. The church must understand that its contribution to the community is greater than the buildings built on Hargrave's campus, or at Samuel Harris Church, or even at the Community Center in the heart of Chatham. The church must reimagine its efforts in building institutions and translate those experiences into building and mending relationships. The church should adapt the same principles of concern, cooperation, and commitment it has used previously to bring its community together, and apply those principles in the future to foster reconciliation. The church can reimagine itself as a catalyst for reconciliation, just as it has been a catalyst for launching community institutions.

The church gathered for worship is how the story of Chatham Baptist Church began in 1857. The church gathered for worship is also the hope for the future of the congregation going forward. In its 1969 handbook, worship was described as "the main objective of our church."[138] In personal interviews with church leaders, they identified "social engagement with each other and the community" as a core church value.[139] However, the church activity held in highest regard by members was worship.[140] One member described gathering for worship as one of our "disciplines of renewal."[141] When worship is infused with the message of love and forgiveness, and those gathered understand that they are gathered together before God who has reconciled each of them to God's own self through Jesus Christ, then the church can begin to dream of extending the ministry of reconciliation to others. When it does that, Chatham Baptist Church will have found its new mission in the twenty-first century.

# CHAPTER 3

# A REVIEW OF SELECT LITERATURE ON RECONCILIATION

The preceding chapters have examined the context of community and church as they relate to a ministry of reconciliation. This chapter shifts attention to academic sources in order to review literature germane to this book's focus. Accordingly, this chapter is bounded by three touchstones which will focus the discussion of the church as a reconciling community.

## Church as a Reconciling Community of Witness

The first of these touchstones argues from ecclesiology that the local church is inherently a reconciling community. Two theologians, both influenced by Anabaptist thought, provide theoretical and practical insight. James McClendon's *Systematic Theology: Doctrine: Volume II* and John Howard Yoder's *Body Politics: Five Practices of the Christian Community before the Watching World* offer ecclesiological contributions to the discussion.

### *Systematic Theology: Doctrine: Volume II* by James William McClendon

In the second of three volumes in his *Systematic Theology*, James McClendon's book, *Doctrine*, contends, "Every Christian theology is written from and for a community."[142] The task McClendon assumes in *Doctrine* is to offer an "unapologetic theology"[143] of an under-represented Christian community which McClendon labels as "baptist," with a lowercase "b." McClendon's "baptist" theology has its roots in the radical reformation of sixteenth-century Anabaptists. However, it extends forward theologically, widening its scope to include Baptist denominations and others in the "free church" or "believers' church" tradition. These "theological successors to

Anabaptism," according to McClendon, "wait in hope to discover that their witness is at least acknowledged in tandem with other witnesses to the one Christ."[144]

While giving voice to a "baptist" theology is McClendon's purpose, the thesis of his book is that the "baptist" community has a distinct perspective to offer the theological world. McClendon argues for a unique "baptist vision" that shapes "baptist" theology and distinguishes it from Catholic and Protestant theologies. This "baptist vision" is captured in the biblical phrase spoken by Peter on Pentecost in Acts 2—"this is that."[145] McClendon quotes Acts 2: 14-16: "But Peter, standing up with the eleven, lifted up his voice, and said unto them, 'Ye men of Judaea, and all ye that dwell at Jerusalem, be this known unto you, and hearken to my words: For these are not drunken, as ye suppose, seeing it is but the third hour of the day. But *this is that* which was spoken by the prophet Joel.'"[146] Using Peter's explanation that the events of Pentecost are a fulfillment of the prophesy of Joel 2:28, McClendon contends that "this is that" constitutes the hermeneutical principle of "baptist" communities. This hermeneutic then forms "a necessary and sufficient organizing principle for a (baptist) theology."[147]

This "baptist vision" is not merely a strategy for Bible reading, according to McClendon, but constitutes "the way" of "Christian existence itself" for "baptists."[148] However, this way is not a "replication of primitive Christian behavior," but rather is a way of acting in a contemporary context based on identification with Jesus' first disciples.[149] Put in other terms, "this is that" takes a biblical event or motif, and applies it "under divine guidance to another set of events and circumstances" in current time and place.[150]

The "baptist vision," therefore, belongs neither to the Catholic nor Protestant streams of Christianity, but constitutes a third type of Christian community, a third understanding of "church."[151] This third way of being in Christian community has several hallmarks. This type of "baptist" community is local in its expression.[152] The term "church" describes the local, gathered assembly,[153] "grounded in Christ's unity with the Father, a unity that entails, creates, ordains *community*."[154] This community is "Spirit-filled, mission-oriented, its discipleship always shaped by a practice of discernment," according to McClendon.[155] Discernment in this case means "spiritual discipline" which takes the "Rule of Christ" from Matthew 18:15 seriously. This rule provided guidance for the assembly of disciples in dealing with errant members of the community, including specific instruction on how to reconcile them back into the community's life.[156]

An example of reconciliation in McClendon's "baptist" ecclesiology is *Doctrine's* approach to the question of the place of the Jews in God's plan. "The Israel of God had been enlarged," McClendon contends. With all "people-in-formation," including Jews, under the "rule of God," the Israel of God is now "a people made out of peoples, a future-oriented, gift-created, plural community of destiny, whose canon or entrance standard is in every case *new creation* (Gal. 6:15)."[157] In summary, the primary contribution of *Doctrine* is its clear picture that the "baptist" vision which provides the cohering center for McClendon's theology encompasses reconciliation as one of the hallmarks of McClendon's "baptist" ecclesiology.

*Doctrine* has self-imposed limitations. For example, it does not explore much in the way of praxis in a reconciling community. While McClendon clearly lays the foundation that a "baptist" church is a reconciling community, the book leaves praxis to others. Despite that limitation, which is both appropriate and necessary in a systematic theology text, *Doctrine* provides the ecclesiological underpinning for developing a community of reconciliation expressed through local church ministry.

## *Body Politics: Five Practices of the Christian Community before the Watching World* by John Howard Yoder

The thesis of John Howard Yoder's book, *Body Politics: Five Practices of the Christian Community before the Watching World*, is that "the people of God is called [sic] to be today what the world is called to be ultimately."[158] For Yoder, a Mennonite theologian, this means that churches demonstrate a "social practice as lived out by early Christians, under divine mandate, which at the same time offers a paradigm for the life of the larger society."[159] In other words, the Church is to demonstrate God's intention for the way the created world should function by living out certain practices "held together by commitment to important values."[160]

Yoder identifies five practices of churches which are demonstrations of God's will for the created world. These practices begin with binding and loosing, which invokes the "rule of Christ."[161] Yoder begins with Matthew 18:15: "If your brother or sister sins, go and point out their fault, just between the two of you. If they listen to you, you have won them over." Yoder contends that when Jesus' disciples carried out this command, "their activity would at the same time be the activity of God." For this assertion Yoder quotes Matthew 18:18, "Truly I tell you, whatever you bind on earth will be bound in heaven, and whatever you loose on earth will be loosed in heaven." Yoder is demonstrating that "the community's action is God's action."[162] Yoder suggests that this redemptive conversation involves "reconciling dialogue . . . moral discernment . . . and, the authority of divine empowerment."[163]

Yoder's concept of "binding and loosing" obviously involves reconciliation as its goal. However, the other four practices Yoder describes touch on reconciliation as well. In the second practice, Yoder reimagines the Eucharistic meal, connecting communion to the "common meal" or table fellowship of the first century. "The Lord's Supper," Yoder argues, "provides ritual leverage for the condemnation of economic segregation."[164] Yoder believes that the Lord's table is an egalitarian one which breaks down barriers, permitting a kind of reconciliation of those formerly estranged from one another and God.

Baptism constitutes Yoder's third practice. Baptism "introduces or initiates persons into a new people," according to Yoder, which means that "the wall between Jew and Gentile has been broken down by the death of Christ." [165] This becomes a reconciling act because baptism, in creating a new people from two estranged groups, relativizes "prior stratifications and classification."[166] Yoder affirms not just the nullification of division, but celebrates the "trans-ethnic unity" that this implies for the Church and "the wider society."[167]

For his fourth practice, Yoder borrows "the fullness of Christ" from Paul's letter to the Ephesians to "describe a new mode of group relationships, in which every member of a body has a distinctly identifiable, divinely validated and empowered role."[168] Yoder contrasts this "multiplicity of gifts" with the current state of Christianity which elevates preachers, priests, bishops, and others to special offices. Yoder contends there is not just "one ministerial role" in a church, but rather, "there are as many ministerial roles as there are members of the body of Christ, and that means more than half of them belong to women."[169] This "multiplicity of gifts" touches the need and possibility for reconciliation between genders in the Church. According to Yoder, "To let a few women into an office that men have for generations wrongly restricted and that did not even exist in the apostolic churches may be a good kind of 'affirmative action,' but it is hardly the most profound vision of renewal."[170]

Yoder's fifth practice is "The Rule of Paul." I Corinthians 12-14 provides the context for Yoder's assertion that Paul means that every member of a church "who has something to say, something given by the Holy Spirit to him or her to say, can have the floor."[171] In similar fashion to the fourth practice, the Rule of Paul affirms the giftedness of each member of the local Christian community. However, it adds the idea that each person has a message from God and should be permitted and encouraged to share that message with the whole community. "Because God the Spirit speaks in the meeting, conversation is the setting for truth-finding," according to Yoder.[172] God's will is known by the Spirit working in the meeting of believers.[173]

While not explicitly written about reconciliation, Yoder's five church practices illustrate the centrality of reconciliation in local church ministry. From church discipline to the communion table, to the worshipping and practicing life of the congregation, Yoder's practices bring together those who were previously estranged. They bridge cultural barriers, and give expression to the unity of the body of Christ. These core practices complement McClendon's "baptist" ecclesiology, providing corresponding focus to McClendon's systematic theology.

Yoder's brief book limits its scope to the five practices described in its subtitle. This sharp focus gives the book clarity, but the book does not cover every discipline, issue, and practice involved in developing a local church reconciliation ministry. Despite the book's limitations, Yoder does provide five compelling practices, basic to most church congregations, in which a church could find elements of reconciliation.

## Reconciliation at the Juncture of Theology, Social Science, and Peace Studies

The second touchstone advocates understanding theology and social sciences as potentially complementary to one another. Often viewed as adversaries, theology informed by social science provides a broad platform for praxis in a local church ministry of reconciliation. David Augsburger's *Helping People Forgive* and John Paul Lederach's *The Moral Imagination: The Art and Soul of Building Peace* will help integrate theology and social science for the community of reconciliation.

### *Helping People Forgive* by David W. Augsburger

David Augsburger's book, *Helping People Forgive*, asserts, "Helping people forgive is our calling, our vocation as persons, whether we are in the 'helping professions' formally, or offering help informally in the daily brushes and abrasions."[174] Augsburger describes the work of an "effective people helper" as a person who "operates from a philosophical position, acts according to an ethical code, treats on the basis of particular personality theories, and functions within a theological world of values."[175] In other words, Augsburger observes the complementarity of philosophy, ethics, psychology, and theology as integral to the task of helping others forgive and reconcile.

The thesis implicit in this volume is that the concepts of forgiveness and reconciliation need "new metaphors" to illustrate their restorative work.[176] The author argues that a different paradigm is needed to understand forgiveness and reconciliation in their multi-faceted expressions. "Forgiveness must be more than social lubricant, survival technique, a relational strategy, a memory fatigue, an individual escape, a dismissal of hurt or anger or a ritual of denial."[177] In these cryptic descriptions, Augsburger is critiquing popular rationales for forgiveness. What forgiveness and reconciliation need, according to Augsburger, is the theological foundation which Jesus offers.[178]

## THE RECONCILING COMMUNITY

Augsburger cites philosopher Hannah Arendt to remind his audience that "Jesus' teaching about forgiveness . . . has been neglected in philosophical and political thought because of its close association with the Christian tradition, but it is a major theological breakthrough."[179] By invoking this observation, Augsburger is calling Christian caregivers back to their theological roots—to the story of Jesus and his teaching. Such teaching shapes worship and prayer, and it calls for a "radical understanding of the forgiving community" in recovering the Christian paradigm of forgiveness and reconciliation.[180]

While theology is essential to the Christian paradigm, it benefits from the insights of philosophy, ethics, and the behavioral sciences for a nuanced understanding. No single definition of forgiveness is possible, according to Augsburger. The practice of forgiveness and reconciliation demands flexibility and openness to a multitude of approaches.[181] In *Helping People Forgive*, Augsburger calls on scholars in the fields of psychology, philosophy, and theology to offer insights into how each of these disciplines can create new paradigms for understanding forgiveness and reconciliation. From the discipline of psychology, Augsburger includes the work of Murray Bowen in family systems theory,[182] Melanie Klein in object relations theory,[183] and Heinz Kohut in narcissistic development theory.[184] From philosophy, Augsburger offers virtue in contrast to the "therapeutic sensibility" of authenticity,[185] and argues, "Virtues of common life depend on the presence of common human social practices, practices that act out the narrative of our lives provided by our community."[186] In addition to Alisdair MacIntyre, Augsburger draws from philosopher René Girard's theory of sacred violence. "True reconciliation," Augsburger contends, "requires that human violence be transformed into suffering; that the innocence of victims be recognized; that guilt and responsibility of violence be faced; and that repentance, rapprochement, and forgiveness be sought."[187]

The book closes its last chapter by locating the work of forgiveness and reconciliation within a community. Augsburger believes that these are clearly communal concepts, and to treat them only as the concern of individuals may result in "satisfactory dispute resolution, not restoration of community."[188] Theologically, we are reconciled to God, and then we are reconciled to one another by God's work. We then become "reconcilers for one another" in a "community of bridge builders."[189] Finally, Augsburger summarizes, "The forgiving community exists within the story of God's forgiveness, lives by the stories of its own participation in forgiveness, and serves as it acts as an agent of forgiveness. To be a participant in a reconciling community is our highest experience of being human and the one undeniable evidence that God is in our midst."[190]

*Helping People Forgive* contributes much to the thesis of this book. Augsburger demonstrates the primacy of Christian theology in the concept of forgiveness and reconciliation. However, he also draws on credible sources from psychology and philosophy to cast light on the complexity of human relationships. By finding complementary ground at the juncture of theology and social science, Augsburger opens the way for a multi-disciplinary approach to forgiveness and reconciliation. In so doing, Augsburger widens the field of resources from which a local church may draw in crafting its own ministry of reconciliation.

*Helping People Forgive* has some limitations for the purpose of this book. Churches seeking to mount a ministry of reconciliation may not need the depth of knowledge that the book presents regarding various psychological perspectives. However, exposure to specific approaches to forgiveness from the field of psychology strengthens the premise that reconciliation is a multi-faceted undertaking.

## *The Moral Imagination: The Art and Soul of Building Peace* by John Paul Lederach

The second resource at the juncture of theology and social sciences is John Paul Lederach's book, *The Moral Imagination: The Art and Soul of Building Peace*. In his book, Lederach addresses the interplay of the creative imagination in the peace-building process. Conceived as a book "that would cut across multiple disciplines,"[191] Lederach argues that the "art of the creative process"[192] often is forgotten in peace studies. A veteran peace builder and respected academic in the field of peace studies,[193] Lederach reflects on his experience, concluding that peace building is "more akin to the artistic endeavor than the technical process."[194]

Lederach's thesis is that "transcending violence is forged by the capacity to generate, mobilize, and build the moral imagination."[195] He defines the moral imagination as "the capacity to imagine something rooted in the challenges of the real world yet capable of giving birth to that which does not yet exist."[196] However, Lederach is not advocating an uninformed approach to peace building. Rather, he is proposing holding both the technical and theoretical insights of peace studies in tension with the "messy and personal process" of real world conditions, situations, and serendipitous moments.[197]

Lederach employs four "guiding stories" as evidence of real situations in which the moral imagination of those involved led to new insights and opportunities in peace building.[198] The first story concerns the ethnic conflict between the Konkomba and Dagomba tribes in Ghana. After recurring violence between the two tribes which threatened to escalate into a full-scale civil war, a humble and respectful appeal from the "nonchiefly" Konkambas' spokesman to the chief of the Dagombas resulted in softening of attitudes and the opening of the peace process.[199]

Lederach titles the second story from Wajir, Kenya, "How a Few Women Stopped a War." In this story, the women of the Wajir region, tired of decades of violence in their area, banded together to establish a "zone of peace" in their local market. Eventually, the women appealed to the region's men, youth, government, schools, and businesses to work together to end the violence through education, jobs, dialogue, and disarmament.[200]

The third story takes place in Colombia, where local workers rejected the false choice of either joining the government militia or joining the rebels. The workers "decided to speak for themselves" rather than have a solution imposed on them. They rejected violence as a means to resolving the region's problems. Banding together in solidarity, the *campesino* leaders asked their neighbors to commit their lives, to "die before we kill," through "lived demonstration of the basic idea that solutions without violence were possible."[201]

Finally, Lederach recounts a story from Tajikistan, where a university professor helps facilitate an end to the Tajikistan civil war. Professor Abdul is appointed the government's emissary to persuade an Islamic commander to enter negotiations. Abdul develops a relationship with this commander over a period of months. The Islamic commander eventually agrees to meet with the government to negotiate on the condition that the professor will guarantee his personal safety at the meeting. Unable to provide that assurance, Professor Abdul instead said to the commander, "But I can guarantee this. I will go with you, side by side. And if you die, I will die." With that personal commitment, the commander agreed to negotiate, and Islamicists were brought into the peace and rebuilding process.[202] In these stories, Lederach contends that neither religion, political power, military might, nor mediation techniques was the key factor in reducing violence and moving toward peace. Rather, Lederach states, "I believe it was the serendipitous appearance of the moral imagination in human affairs."[203]

The contribution of *The Moral Imagination* to this book is best described in Lederach's own words: "What if reconciliation were more like a creative artistic process than a linear formula of cumulative activities aimed a producing a result?" The book appeals to readers to acknowledge, cultivate, and watch for signs of the moral imagination in seeking to bring reconciliation to estranged groups. Integrating biblical references, Lederach quotes from both Old and New Testaments to give theological foundation to his observations.[204] Moreover, Lederach's own theological commitment as a Mennonite provides the understated theology behind this work. Lederach sums up his understanding of the "theology of mystery" in the lives of those he has studied who were involved in peace-building processes. He writes, "They had ventured on a journey toward a land totally unfamiliar. Exploration of that unknown land called peace building, I thought, was akin to the mysterious journey toward the sacred. It is the same land, I have come to believe, that the moral imagination requires us to explore."[205]

The limitations of the book are acknowledged by the author in his preface. Lederach states, "I wish to hold myself close to the actual messiness of ideas, processes, and change and from such a place speculate about the nature of our work and the lessons learned."[206] *The Moral Imagination* offers an insightful, experiential foray into the world of peace building by valuing the creative insights necessary to form a community committed to reconciliation.

## Models for Practicing Reconciliation in and Through Community

The third touchstone explores literature relating to models for practicing reconciliation within different types of communities. Gregory Jones examines forgiveness as craft in the Christian church in his book, *Embodying Forgiveness: A Theological Analysis*. Bryant L. Myers offers insights into community development and reconciliation in *Walking with the Poor: Principles and Practices of Transformational Development*. Finally, Ani Kalayjian and Raymond F. Paloutzian edit a volume of case studies titled *Forgiveness and Reconciliation: Psychological Pathways to Conflict Transformation and Peace Building*. These three books provide a diverse look at how various communities have addressed the practice of reconciliation.

### *Embodying Forgiveness: A Theological Analysis* by L. Gregory Jones

In *Embodying Forgiveness: A Theological Analysis*, Gregory Jones argues that the Trinity is the context in which forgiveness is situated. As such, Jones posits, "God's love moves toward reconciliation by means of costly forgiveness."[207] The result of God's action is "human beings are called to become holy by embodying that forgiveness through specific habits and practices that seek to remember the past truthfully; to repair the brokenness, to heal divisions, and to reconcile and renew relationships."[208]

From Jones's viewpoint, forgiveness is not just a "word spoken or a feeling felt" so much as it is a way of life embodied in the community called the Church. Contrary to popular therapeutic notions of forgiveness, Jones contends that forgiveness should be focused on "reconciliation of brokenness, the restoration of communion—with God, with one another, and with the whole Creation."[209] The forgiveness and reconciliation Jones describes finds expression in the "craft of forgiveness that Christians are called to learn from one another."[210] This forgiveness is not just theological and theoretical, but consists of "habits, practices, friendship, craft."[211]

Jones decries the "church's psychological captivity in Western culture" by arguing that the Western Church and her leaders have been seduced by the therapeutic notions of psychology and self-help remedies. Jones argues, "We find forgiveness not by looking within our selves [sic] but by being restored to communion with God and with one another in and through specific practices of forgiveness."[212] Lewis Smedes, author of the popular book, *Forgive and Forget: Healing the Hurts We Don't Deserve*, suffers a withering critique by Jones. Smedes, Jones asserts, "oversimplifies the very description of why forgiveness is necessary." In contrast to Jones's position, "Smedes's description internalizes and privatizes forgiveness so that there is little need for its embodiment in specific places."[213]

Jones grounds his theological analysis of forgiveness in an exploration of the triune God—the Father who wills communion, and thereby reconciliation;[214] the Son who demonstrates messianic forgiveness, while shifting forgiveness from the Temple in Jerusalem to communities of disciples;[215] and, the Spirit who "listens, judges, and guides believers" in living lives of forgiveness.[216] As part of a faith community, believers find new meaning in the practices of baptism, communion, and reconciling forgiveness.[217]

Finally, Jones explores the "craft of forgiveness" and asserts, "It is God's forgiveness, not interhuman forgiveness, that ought to provide the contours for our understanding of forgiveness."[218] The craft of forgiveness has some characteristics, however. First, it features "truthful judgment" about the situation. Secondly, those involved must possess a "willingness to acknowledge both the propriety of anger, resentment, or bitterness" along with the desire to move beyond them. Third, a "concern for the well-being of other(s) as children of God" motivates forgiveness in community. Fourth, awareness of the "ways in which we all need to be forgiven" offers perspective on the common human condition. Fifth, the community acknowledges that "truthful judgment requires accountability directed toward the grace for new life." Finally, "the hope for eventual reconciliation" provides incentive for forgiveness to be practiced.[219] Jones offers these six characteristics, not as steps or "stages" of forgiveness, but as "themes that interact in different ways in the craft of forgiveness."[220]

*Embodying Forgiveness* contributes much to the thesis of this book. First, Jones offers a robust theological foundation for forgiveness and reconciliation. Secondly, the book differentiates this theological ground from the therapeutic and popular psychology models that have made forgiveness into a private, unilateral act which may or may not lead to reconciliation. Finally, Jones draws a picture of forgiveness as a craft which belongs to particular communities of faith. Jones's argument builds a firm theological foundation for the craft of forgiveness, situates it within the life of the triune God, and then explicates its characteristics in community practice.

The book's limitation, for the purpose of this book, lies in the caution that the therapeutic and the theological are at odds. While Jones argues for the Church to recover its own theological language and practice of forgiveness, he leaves little room for the theology of forgiveness to be informed by the practices of psychology. However, the strength of Jones's book is its theological explication of forgiveness and reconciliation, and their location in the local church as a forgiving, reconciling community.

## *Walking with the Poor: Principles and Practices of Transformational Development* by Bryant L. Myers

The next book to touch on the theme of reconciliation within the context of community is Bryant L. Myers's work, *Walking with the Poor: Principles and Practices of Transformational Development*. Myers's book describes "a proposal for understanding the principles and practice of transformational development (positive material, social, and spiritual change) from a Christian perspective."[221] While Myers's thesis is not focused specifically on reconciliation, the nature of transformative development incorporates elements necessary for any organization to become an agent of reconciliation.

The overall scope of the book surveys each facet of what Myers labels *transformative development*. For Myers that phrase means "concern for seeking positive change in the whole of human life materially, socially, and spiritually."[222] Rather than separating the spiritual from the physical, transformative development unites them. Myers contends, "God's rule extends to both the spiritual and material."[223] To ground his thesis theologically, Myers begins with "The Biblical Story" in Chapter 1. It is in this story that a helpful framework for understanding a community's story is found. The biblical story explains how every community's story began and why its story is full of pain, injustice, and struggle at the same time that it is "full of joy, loving relationships, and hope."[224]

The main theme of the biblical story is "ultimately about relationships, restored relationships," according to Myers. Relationships must be restored in the four categories in which they have been alienated: with God, with others, with those who are "other" to us, and with Creation.[225] Quoting Nicholas Wolterstorff, Myers invokes the biblical concept of shalom to expand on this argument. "First, shalom is a relational concept, 'dwelling at peace with God, with self, with fellows, and with nature.'"[226] *Shalom* also includes

> just relationships (living justly and experiencing justice), harmonious relationships, and enjoyable relationships. Shalom means belonging to an authentic and nurturing community in which one can be one's true self and give one's self away without becoming poor. Justice, harmony, and enjoyment of God, self, others, and nature; this is the shalom that Jesus brings, the peace that passes all understanding.[227]

Perhaps most helpful are the ways in which Myers challenges the conventional wisdom about poverty, the poor, and the role of the community developer. Poverty is more than a deficit of material possessions, Myers argues.[228] Poverty entangles the poor in a "poverty trap," which has implications for their material well-being, their physical health condition, their access to a society's basic services and information, their ability to buffer against hardship, their inability to influence life events and circumstances, and their "relationships with God, each other, the community, and creation."[229]

After examining various models of community development, Myers offers these goals for transformational development with its Christian perspective: "changed people" and "just and peaceful relationships."[230] To achieve that goal, practitioners need to develop eleven characteristics. According to Myers, the holistic practitioner strives to be "a good neighbor" with a willingness to listen and change himself or herself; "patient" with the pace of transformation progress; and "humble before the facts" because others know more than is often expected, and new facts become evident. In addition, practitioners should recognize that "everyone is learning" in the process, that "everywhere is holy" because God was in the community before the practitioner, and that "every moment and every action is potentially transforming."[231] Myers also lists "loving people and not the program," loving the local churches already present in the community, cultivating repentance and forgiveness, exhibiting trust in God rather than programs or expertise, and valuing the perception of those with whom the practitioner is working.[232]

Clearly Myers has provided significant practical and applicable insights, not only in terms of transformational development, but also in terms of the underlying premise that restored (or reconciled) relationships are at the core of his view of development. Myers challenges practitioners to watch for their own biases, to listen to the people with whom they are working, to explore the history of the community in which they hope transformation comes, and to undergird all of that with a clear theological sensibility. Local churches hoping to engage in reconciliation practices would find much that is helpful in Myers's book.

The limitations of *Walking with the Poor* primarily lie in the book's stated focus and audience. However, with careful reading the text allows itself to be translated into the language of reconciliation. Communities are not just poor in material resources; they are also poor in spiritual resources. Myers's book provides a wealth of support for those seeking transformation of their own communities through the restoration of relationships.

### *Forgiveness and Reconciliation: Psychological Pathways to Conflict Transformation and Peace Building* by Ani Kalayjian and Raymond F. Paloutzian, editors

The final book in this section concerning reconciliation in and through community is *Forgiveness and Reconciliation: Psychological Pathways to Conflict Transformation and Peace Building*, edited by Ani Kalayjian and Raymond F. Paloutzian. The editors describe the book as exploring "forgiveness, reconciliation, and related topics at multiple levels, from individual and group, to intergroup relations."[233]

The book is divided into three sections. Section I deals with the theoretic aspects of forgiveness and reconciliation as they relate to systemic violence and peace building.[234] Section II covers individual and interpersonal theory and practice in forgiveness and reconciliation.[235] Section III expands the focus of the book to "intergroup, societal, and international levels" by using case studies from different societies and nations that have experienced widespread conflict. Rwanda, Darfur, the India-Pakistan conflict, and the Armenia genocide provide historical examples of each conflict, and the efforts at forgiveness and reconciliation attempted in each instance.[236]

The primary contribution of this volume to the thesis of this book is to illustrate that reconciliation is not only a transaction between individuals, but also is applicable to larger groups, societies, and nation-states. This insight will be helpful to Chatham Baptist Church, and to other local churches which might become involved in various ministries of reconciliation within their own context. In addition to the case studies, the book offers a theoretical foundation from the discipline of peace psychology studies. Although *Forgiveness and Reconciliation* reflects a multidisciplinary perspective,[237] the book acknowledges and explores the role of world religions in the psychology of forgiveness and reconciliation. The authors and editors ask tough questions such as "How do religions foster characteristics that facilitate forgiveness?" and "How might religions impede processes of forgiveness?"[238] The authors and editors clearly understand that religion can and does play a significant role in reconciliation. The book also cautions that religious bodies can be forces that facilitate or inhibit forgiveness and reconciliation in groups, societies, and nations.[239]

The limitations of *Forgiveness and Reconciliation* for the purposes of this book are inherent in the book's premise that reconciliation can scale up from taking place on an individual level to taking place on intergroup, societal, national, and international levels. Most local churches in the United States, including Chatham Baptist Church, will not be involved in national or international peace-building efforts. However, the study of reconciliation as a means to peace building in wider contexts will encourage local churches engaged in reconciling ministry to see themselves as part of a larger, worldwide peace building community.

In conclusion, these seven books anchor three basic concepts for the local church engaged in a ministry of reconciliation. First, a church is a theologically appropriate locus for reconciling efforts. Second, other disciplines can inform a church's theology as it crafts a local strategy for reconciliation. Finally, reconciliation is possible between individuals, groups, and nations. No conflict or hurt is so large or so small that it cannot be attended to by those who wish to offer forgiveness and reconciliation.

# CHAPTER 4

# THEOLOGY OF THE CHURCH REIMAGINED

Exploring ecclesiology at Chatham Baptist Church takes up the "main task of theology: to reflect on and make sense of what is happening in Christian life and churches."[240] To accomplish that purpose, the first section of this chapter will present five historic Baptist ecclesiological principles identified by Baptist historians. The second part will critique these principles for weaknesses that might inhibit the transformation of Chatham Baptist Church into a reconciling community. In the third section an alternative vision of church life from the Anabaptist perspective will be examined. Finally, section four features a reimagined ecclesiology informed by Anabaptist theology which will more effectively enable a ministry of reconciliation at Chatham Baptist Church.

### Historic Church Characteristics in Southern Baptist Life

Baptists as a theological community have not produced "a theological literature in proportion to that of other denominations," according to James McClendon.[241] As a result, discerning Baptist ecclesiological principles requires a look at Baptist history. In his book, *The Baptist Identity: Four Fragile Freedoms*, Walter Shurden identifies four principles, or "freedoms," which describe Baptist ecclesiological emphases. Shurden identifies these "freedoms" by analyzing sermons and s presented at meetings of the Baptist World Alliance from its founding in 1905 through 1989.[242]

The first of these five principles is "soul freedom," which has also been called "'the competency of the soul before God," "personal faith," and "soul liberty."[243] In 1908, Southern Baptist theologian E. Y. Mullins popularized the "doctrine of the soul's competency in religion under God" with the publication of his book, *The Axioms of Religion*. Mullins asserted that "soul competency" was the signature historical contribution of Baptists to the wider theological world.[244] Mullins believed that from "soul freedom" flowed all the other hallmarks of Baptist life—the sovereignty of God, "the equal right of human beings to access to God," and the right of believers to equal standing in the Church.[245] Shurden defines "soul freedom" as "the historic Baptist affirmation of the inalienable right and responsibility of every person to deal with God without imposition of creed, the interference of clergy, or the intervention of civil government."[246]

This principle is the "primary axiom of Baptist faith and practice," according to Baptist historian, David Bebbington.[247] "Soul freedom" finds expression when an individual who has reached "the age at which it is possible for persons to come to faith on their own"[248] professes faith in Christ personally, is baptized into a local church, and takes his or her place in the congregation. The believer's privileges include the right to vote in democratic congregational meetings,[249] to interpret Scripture personally,[250] to participate in missions and evangelism,[251] and to be a peer among peers in membership.[252] Shurden concludes his chapter on "soul freedom" by defining it succinctly: "The individual is central. The Christian faith is personal, experiential, and voluntary.'"[253]

The second freedom which Shurden proposes is "church freedom." Shurden defines "church freedom" as "the historic Baptist affirmation that local churches are free, under the Lordship of Christ, to determine their membership and leadership, to order their worship and work, to ordain whom they perceive as gifted for ministry, male or female, and to participate in the larger Body of Christ, of whose unity and mission Baptists are proudly a part."[254] In 1963 Southern Baptists adopted a statement of faith titled *The Baptist Faith and Message*.[255] The section on "The Church" states, "A New Testament church of the Lord Jesus Christ is a local body of baptized believers who are associated by covenant in the faith and fellowship of the gospel. . . . This church is an autonomous body, operating through democratic processes under the lordship of Jesus Christ."[256] Herschel

Hobbs, a primary author of *The Baptist Faith and Message*, notes in his commentary, "The word 'church' in the New Testament never refers to organized Christianity or to a group of churches. It denotes either a local body of baptized believers or includes all the redeemed of all the ages. The greater emphasis among Baptists, as in the New Testament, is on the local church."[257]

From the beginning Southern Baptists have maintained fiercely independent local congregations, but these autonomous churches quickly formed "associations" of "like-minded Baptist churches" to work together on their common interest of missions.[258] However cooperation with outsiders is limited in Southern Baptist life by the concept that "church" is defined first and foremost as a local congregation. In 1940 the SBC rejected an invitation to participate in the World Council of Churches on the grounds that "The Southern Baptist Convention was 'in no sense the Southern Baptist Church'; hence it could not become a member of a 'fellowship of churches.'"[259]

The third freedom Shurden lists is "Bible freedom."[260] Baptists have described themselves as "people of the Book."[261] *The Baptist Faith and Message* of 1963, to which Chatham Baptist Church subscribes, accords first place to a section on "The Scriptures."[262]

Bible freedom for Southern Baptists has four facets, according to Shurden. First, Bible freedom means "Christians stand . . . with an open Bible 'under' the Lordship of Jesus Christ."[263] Second, Baptists historically have sought to win and retain "freedom of access to the Bible 'for' the purpose of continuing obedience to the Word of God."[264] Third, Bible freedom means Baptists are free "from" having creedal statements imposed on them by any individual or group. Finally, Baptists exercise their right "of" individual interpretation of Scripture. Shurden acknowledges that the "absence of any single, final or official interpretation of scripture has created diversity, consternation, and even conflict between Baptists themselves."[265] Despite past controversies, the Bible continues to play the central authoritative role in Southern Baptist life.

"Religious freedom" is the fourth of Shurden's freedoms. *The Baptist Faith and Message* section on "Religious Liberty" states in part,

"Church and state should be separate. . . . A free church in a free state is the Christian ideal, and this implies the right of free and unhindered access to God on the part of all men, and the right to form and propagate opinions in the sphere of religion without interference by the civil power."[266] Shurden defines religious freedom as "the historic Baptist affirmation of freedom OF religion, freedom FOR religion, and freedom FROM religion, insisting that Caesar is not Christ and Christ is not Caesar."[267]

According to renowned Southern Baptist leader, George W. Truett, "Baptists have one consistent record concerning liberty throughout all their long and eventful history."[268] Although Anabaptists originated the concept of religious liberty,[269] Baptists in America brought the issue to the forefront during the nation's nascence. Roger Williams, Isaac Backus, and John Leland are representative of those who advocated religious liberty from the 1630s to the 1840s. Virginia pastor John Leland wrote. "The liberty I contend for, is more than toleration. The very idea of toleration, is despicable; it supposes that some have a pre-eminence above the rest, to grant indulgence; whereas, all should be equally free, Jews, Turks, Pagans and Christians."[270]

The fifth and final mark of Southern Baptist ecclesiology is the understanding that the mission of every SBC church is "missions," or global evangelization. Southern Baptists believe they are charged to carry out Christ's Great Commission found in Matthew 28:19-20: "Therefore go and make disciples of all nations." *The Baptist Faith and Message* section on "The Church" concludes that Baptist churches are "to extend the gospel to the ends of the earth."[271] This conviction, shared by Baptists worldwide, was delineated in a Baptist World Alliance paper titled, "Towards a Baptist Identity," which contained five defining principles. Shurden restated the first four of these principles as "Bible freedom," "soul freedom," "church freedom," and "religious freedom."[272] The fifth principle states, "Baptists are those who believe that the Great Commission to take the Gospel to the whole world is the responsibility of the whole membership."[273]

"The heartbeat of the Southern Baptist Convention is missions," observes W. R. Estep.[274] In 1845 Baptists in the South split with Baptists in the North because northerners refused to appoint slave-holding southerners as missionaries. The offended Southerners formed the SBC to allow their appointment. Commenting on the founding of the SBC, Estep glosses over slavery to focus on missions: "Missions became its [the SBC's] primary reason for being. A difference over the slavery issue had divided—missions united."275

Southern Baptists continue to promote the missions mandate of "The Great Commission" as the preeminent work of the denomination. At the 2012 meeting of the SBC, messengers voted to retain the legal name of "The Southern Baptist Convention," despite its regional ties. However it was recommended that SBC churches use the informal alternative, "Great Commission Baptists," in settings where "Southern" has negative connotations. Proponents argued that the name "Great Commission Baptists" would give the SBC advantages in evangelism and racial reconciliation.276

## Weaknesses in Southern Baptist Ecclesiology

Despite their influence on denominational life, the five historic principles that have shaped Southern Baptist ecclesiology exhibit inherent weaknesses. Southern Baptists and others have critiqued the five principles described in the previous section. Identifying the weaknesses which might inhibit the transformation of Chatham Baptist Church into a reconciling community is a primary concern of this section.

The first principle, "soul freedom," has been characterized as a kind of hyper-individualism. No sooner had Mullins asserted soul competency in his book, *The Axioms of Religion*, than criticism began. Mullins grounded "soul competency" in individual "religious experience," contending it was "the starting point for theological reflection."277 Influenced by Friedrich Schleiermacher's "experiential-based methodology," Mullins insisted that his focus on the individual was based on the New Testament, not modern liberalism.278 Despite Mullins's disavowals, Winthrop Hudson observed wryly that Mullins's "soul competency" had the effect of making "everyman's hat his own church."279 Harold Bloom, professor of humanities at Yale University, writes that "Soul competency . . . has in it an element of isolation and of intense individuation. It is a very rough version of Emersonian self-reliance."[280] James McClendon asserts that "'soul competency' was framed too much in terms of the rugged American individualism of Theodore Roosevelt to do justice to the shared discipleship baptist life requires."[281]

A major drawback to over-emphasizing individual faith experience is that doing so minimizes the role of the faith community. In addition, reconciliation is reduced to a transaction between individuals or between an individual and God, with little regard to the role and function of the faith community in the process. This contradicts the emphasis on community promoted by authors cited in Chapter 3 like McClendon, Yoder, Augsburger, and Jones.

The weakness of the second principle called "church freedom" is isolationism brought about by an emphasis on local church autonomy. While this emphasis allows local churches to "determine their own membership and leadership, to order their worship and work, to ordain whom they perceive as gifted for ministry, male or female, and to participate in the larger Body of Christ,"[282] historic examples contradict Shurden's assertion that Baptists eagerly work with others. In addition to declining the invitation of the World Council of Churches, the SBC also withdrew support from the Baptist World Alliance in 2004. Ironically, the Baptist World Alliance is a global Baptist organization that the SBC was instrumental in the founding in 1905. However, ninety-nine years later the SBC's stated reasons for withdrawal from the Baptist World Alliance indicated a narrowing of theology and fellowship. Reasons for SBC withdrawal included "a continual leftward drift," "anti-American stances," some member denominations which question the "inerrancy and infallibility of Scriptures," and the Baptist World Alliance's admission of a Baptist association which contained two churches sympathetic to "gay marriage."[283]

Other Baptist voices have advocated for a more inclusive approach. McClendon suggests that Baptists must acknowledge "the grace of God in places other than our place, in persons other than ourselves, in churches other than our churches."[284] Baptists in Great Britain recognize that "although each local church is held to be competent, under Christ, to rule its own life, Baptists, throughout their history, have been aware of the perils of isolation and have sought safeguards against exaggerated individualism."[285]

The tendency of isolationism in the principle of "church freedom" is devastating to the pursuit of a ministry of reconciliation. Isolationism devalues others outside the Baptist circle. It is the kind of "go it alone" attitude that inhibited racial harmony and delayed for 150 years an apology for slavery from Southern Baptists.[286]

The third Baptist principle of "Bible freedom"—the individual's solitary right to interpret Scripture—is subject to critique because of its inherent subjectivism. Surprisingly, Baptists who claim fidelity to the Bible have not agreed always on how it is to be understood and interpreted.[287] The most recent Baptist controversy over the Bible began in 1979 and roiled the SBC for several years. This controversy did not concern whether or not the "Bible alone is God's word," but "whether the original, non-extant Hebrew and Greek manuscripts of the Bible were without errors in matters of science and history as well as faith and morals."[288] Despite the controversy, however, Baptists on both sides continued to "insist that to the best of their ability they understand their beliefs and practices to mirror those of the New Testament church."[289] Although Southern Baptists have maintained that the Bible is the sole authority in matters of faith and practice, they have had difficulty with its definition and interpretation.[290]

In Baptist history, the principle of "Bible freedom" does not require that the person interpreting Scripture have any training. For Baptists, conversion alone qualifies a person to interpret the Bible for himself or herself under the guiding illumination of the Holy Spirit.[291] Harold Bloom borrows imagery from a beloved evangelical hymn, *In the Garden*, to illustrate Baptist individualism in religion, including biblical interpretation: "Nothing that I have perceived of the American Religion is more persuasive than the image of the Southern Baptist alone in the garden with Jesus."[292] David Augsburger labels this "me and Jesus" faith[293] as "bipolar spirituality" because of its exclusive focus on God and the individual.[294]

The problems attendant to individual interpretation of the Bible could be mitigated by McClendon's vision for a new Baptist identity. McClendon posits "Bible Study in reading communities rather than relying on private interpretation."[295] Randy Hatchett also affirms a "hermeneutics of community."[296] Terry Carter argues persuasively that the use of Scripture as justification for slavery left a legacy of racial prejudice which played out in Southern Baptist life for 150 years.[297] In short, while Baptists may be "people of the Book," it takes a faithful community to discern, understand, and live out the Bible's teachings.

The fourth Baptist principle of "religious freedom" appears to be completely intact. In the United States, the *Bill of Rights* guarantees that "Congress shall make no law respecting an establishment of religion, or prohibiting the free exercise thereof."[298] However, Shurden warns of dangers to religious liberty, not from its loss to atheists or agnostics, but because of its abuse by those who possess it, Baptists included.[299] Shurden poses questions to his Baptist audience to alert them to the possibility of compromising the liberty Baptists historically suffered to win: "But what now? What about Baptists today? Having become prominent and powerful, especially in the United States, are we still as committed to religious liberty for all persons as our ancestors were? And does this include those outside the Judeo-Christian tradition? Do we believe in the separation of church and state as much as we did in a day when it worked against us?"[300] Shurden cites as threats to religious liberty the extreme Reconstruction Movement which promotes a theocratic United States government; he also cites the confusion of citizenship and discipleship among fundamentalists who advocate reinstituting prayer in public schools, using tax dollars to support religious institutions, and having government-sanctioned religious symbols in the public square.[301]

Along the same lines, "religious freedom" can also become corrupted by cultural trends and forces. Norman Kraus situates Southern Baptists within American evangelicalism.[302] Kraus notes that "evangelical theology has no clear-cut critique of American culture. Its theology and ethics continue to be closely allied with a nationalistic political rationale."[303] Mark Noll, in his book *American Evangelical Christianity*, suggests that Southern Baptists have played a significant role in the right-ward political shift of evangelical Protestants:

> The movement of the South from a mainstay of the Democratic Party to an active shaper of the Republican party—and during a period when the largest conservative Protestant denomination in the South, the Southern Baptist Convention, has witnessed a successful effort by self-styled conservatives to control their denomination—has contributed greatly to evangelical political mobilization in the nation as a whole.[304]

Fisher Humphreys, a moderate Baptist, laments the shifting position of Southern Baptists regarding religious liberty. Humphreys writes, "The loss of the principle of the separation of church and state is the greatest theological disaster in the history of the Southern Baptist Convention."[305] William Brackney observes that some Baptists might be unaware of their "heritage in matters pertaining to religious liberty."[306] Brackney believes that these Baptists are "not as concerned about [religious] freedom as with their task to create a cultural Christianity."[307]

Finally, confusing "missions" with the Church's mission is a primary weakness in Southern Baptist ecclesiology and demonstrates outmoded thinking about the Church's mission. In their book, *Missional Church: A Vision for the Sending of the Church in North America*, the authors argue that "it has taken us decades to realize that mission is not just a program of the church. It defines the church as God's sent people. Either we are defined by mission, or we reduce the scope of the gospel and the mandate of the church. Thus our challenge today is to move from church with mission to missional church."[308] However, the authors acknowledge that "congregations still tend to view missions as one of several programs of the church. . . . The sending-receiving mentality is still strong as churches collect funds and send them off to genuine mission enterprises elsewhere."[309] As noted in Chapter 2, Chatham Baptist Church has participated in this collecting-and-sending effort for its entire history, largely because this is the way in which "missions" has been promoted historically in Southern Baptist life.

However, being a missional church involves more than evangelistic missions. In their book, *Introducing the Missional Church*, Alan Roxburgh and Scott Boren write, "God's dream for the world is about redemption of all creation, not just individuals getting into heaven; it is about the restoration of life as God intended it to be; it is about realigning life around God and God's ways."[310] This wider understanding of the church's mission as more than world evangelization creates space for spiritual and social reconciliation among individuals and groups.

## An Alternative Ecclesiology for a Reconciling Community

Despite its accomplishments as a denomination, the SBC's historic church principles have obvious flaws. However, Anabaptist ecclesiology offers an appealing alternative to the weaknesses inherent in Southern Baptist life. In order to examine Anabaptist counterpoints to all five Baptist principles, the writings of contemporary Mennonite theologians will be examined.

First, the Anabaptist concept of the individual's faith commitment differs from that of Southern Baptists. Rather than an abstract concept of "soul freedom," Anabaptists understand "the essence of Christianity as discipleship."[311] This means that the focus is not on the individual's faith, but on his or her following Christ in daily living.[312] This following of Christ with others is made possible because each person is an "individual-in-community," according to C. Norman Kraus.[313] In addition, writes Kraus, "Human beings express the image [of God] through their participation as persons in human community."[314] In contrast to the Southern Baptist evangelical vision, the Anabaptist vision means that Jesus' ministry "was not a ministry of releasing individuals from the web of physical and social relationships through inner spiritual enlightenment," explains Kraus; rather, Jesus "called individuals to new dimensions of self-awareness and personhood in the new covenant community."[315]

The implications of the "individual-in-community" for a ministry of reconciliation in a local church are almost self-evident. First, the ministry of reconciliation belongs to the whole community, not just to one or two persons. Previously cited works by Gregory Jones and David Augsburger would concur with that viewpoint. Secondly, the "rule of Christ" from Matthew 18:15 can find expression in congregations when the entire church takes reconciliation as its corporate work. Finally, Kraus contends that "salvation involves not only isolated individuals in relation to God, but also in the creation of community under God."[316] Kraus further states, "There is no more possibility of personal identity in Christ apart from the brother or sister than there is of loving Christ without loving them."[317] The ministry of reconciliation, when owned by the entire community of faith, becomes a reflection of the reconciliation Christ's followers have experienced through Christ, and their incorporation into a new community of the Spirit.

Secondly, in contrast to Baptist "church freedom," where independent individuals voluntarily associate in an autonomous congregation, Anabaptists posit a "tripolar spirituality" that involves God, the individual, and their neighbor. This triangular relationship believes that love for neighbor is evidence of love for God.[318] Individuals who love God and neighbor are incorporated into a new community, and are therefore individuals-in-community. This new community gathers for worship to prepare it for participation in God's "mission to the world."[319] In contrast to the absence of a worship reference in the *Baptist Faith and Message*, Mennonites value worship "as the communal cultivation of an alternative structure of society and history."[320] As such, worship provides a "truthful encounter with God, who loves the world, and who wants to empower his people to participate in his mission to the world."[321]

In their book, *A Culture of Peace*, Alan Kreider, Eleanor Kreider, and Paulus Widjaja describe the Mennonite worship experience. In worship, the faith community meets "other people in God's presence." In so doing, worship accomplishes several tasks. First, believers gather "'in Jesus' name to confess that Jesus is Lord.'"[322] Worshippers also "affirm solidarity" with the larger Christian community, "God's global family."[323] In worship, those gathered "remember God's story," the metanarrative through which the community sees "reality and upon which we arrange, explain, analyze, and interpret moral precepts."[324] God also reconciles and forgives the worshipping community so that it can pass on reconciliation and forgiveness to the world. Worshippers then "cry out to God for the world."[325] It is at this point in worship that worshippers move from their own relationship with God to "entering the work of God" in the world.[326] For Mennonites, "church freedom" means they are free to encounter God, love their neighbors, and participate in God's plan for all of God's creation.

Third, the Baptist idea of "Bible freedom" is transformed from an individual's right to interpret Scripture alone, to the call of an individual-in-community to live out Scripture by following Jesus in daily living. Even though the Bible is central to Anabaptism, it is a primarily seen as "a witness to Jesus Christ."[327] Scripture is read with Jesus at the center, often beginning with the Sermon on the Mount. This is neither a "flat reading" of the Bible as though all parts of it were equal,[328] nor is it a reading based on theories of inspiration or infallibility.[329] Rather, the Anabaptist hermeneutic presupposes three positions, as delineated by Ted Grimsrud in his book, *Embodying the Way of Jesus*. First, "Anabaptist hermeneutics is the hermeneutics of obedience." Second, "Anabaptists affirm 'the hermeneutical privilege of the poor.'" Finally, "The congregation provides the most fundamental context for biblical interpretation."[330] From this understanding of the Bible, Anabaptists function as a contrast community, living in nonconformity to the rest of the world. This "separation" from the ways of the world does not mean withdrawal from engagement with the world, however. Anabaptists see their living out of the demands of discipleship as serving a "transforming (not withdrawing) agenda."[331]

Fourth, rather than the Baptist idea of "religious freedom" and its subsequent identification with conservative Americanism, Anabaptists have their own community narratives. According to Harold Bender's *The Anabaptist Vision*, "The Anabaptist movement was one of the most tragic in the history of Christianity; but, judged by the principles . . . it must be pronounced one of the most momentous and significant undertakings in man's eventful religious struggle after truth."[332] Bender defines this movement in three parts. First, the "conception of the essence of Christianity as discipleship" was a radical new idea introduced into the mix of the Protestant Reformation.[333] Secondly, Anabaptists created a new concept of the Church governed "by the central principle of newness of life and applied Christianity."[334] Finally, the "ethic of love and nonresistance as applied to all human relationships" meant the "complete abandonment of all warfare, strife, and violence, and of the taking of human life."[335]

These stories and the concepts on which they were based form a more compelling narrative of "experience, Scripture, and community"[336] than the story of Southern Baptist beginnings as apologists for slavery. Mennonite theologian Harry Huebner comments on stories he heard as a boy growing up as a Mennonite:

> These stories made me immensely proud. The message I got as a little boy on hearing them went something like this: "My people know what they believe and take their convictions to be ultimately true. They are not about to sacrifice their identity for an expedient end, won at the threat of death. Wow, this is who I am: these are my stories. I can (want to) participate in them by putting on the character that makes such stories mine!" Although I was not involved in any of them I experienced these stories as being about me.[337]

The story of "Anabaptist-Mennonite history," according to Grimsrud, "is filled with illustrations of this brotherhood and 'Good Samaritan' faith in action."[338]

Finally, rather than the local church's mission being "missions," Mennonite churches are peace communities, seeking to bring God's shalom to the world.[339] According to John Howard Yoder,

> But what matters most, the real reason God lets time go on, is his calling together of his own people through the witness of the gospel. Not building and protecting a bigger and better democracy, but building the church is God's purpose; not the defeat of communism, or of hunger, but the proclamation of his kingdom and the welding of all kinds of men and women into one body is what we are here for.[340]

If building the Church is God's purpose, then the Church is to announce that the "reign of God as proclaimed by Jesus is that shalom which was promised in the later Old Testament writings as a gift of God."[341] Perry Yoder summarizes the connection between church and shalom: "Shalom makers thus strive for total reconciliation—among people, putting an end to want, oppression, and deception; and between people and God, so that all can live in the newness of life that is the vision of shalom."[342]

In describing God's vision for the church, Kreider, Kreider, and Widjaja, suggest that churches are supposed to create a "culture of peace" within their ministry contexts. As an illustration of reconciliation, the authors cite Acts 10, which contains Peter's mission to the house of Cornelius, where Peter announces "the good news of peace" which had come to Gentiles as well as Jews.[343]

## Reimagining Southern Baptist Ecclesiology in Light of the Influence of Anabaptist Thought and Practice

Chatham Baptist Church was founded as a Southern Baptist congregation in 1857, and it remains so today. While the church continues to affirm the *Baptist Faith and Message* of 1963, and does not embrace changes in Southern Baptist ecclesiology as found in the *Baptist Faith and Message* adopted by the Convention in 2000, it remains a cooperating Southern Baptist church. Despite the weaknesses in the five Baptist ecclesiological principles, Chatham Baptist Church will not completely reject those principles, nor will it leave the Baptist denomination to embrace Mennonite ecclesiology. However, in order to facilitate a ministry of reconciliation within its community, Chatham Baptist Church can reimagine the five Baptist principles in light of the influence of Anabaptist theology. The church would then craft an ecclesiology more conducive to its becoming a reconciling community.

First, rather than the hyper-individualism of Mullins's "soul competency," the Chatham Baptist congregation might imagine itself as a faith community gathered around Jesus and sent by him into the world. Three components combine to shape this viewpoint.

First, rather than being a collection of individuals, the church is seen as primarily a community like the church of the New Testament, and the nation of Israel in the Old Testament. Persons are not "autonomous" agents, but are "individuals-in-community" who relate to God both as separate persons, and as God's collective people. Secondly, the phrase "gathered around Jesus" provides an authoritative focus and practice for the congregation. Its first obligation is to its Lord and Savior, Jesus Christ, as the revelation of God incarnate. The person of Jesus is the focus of worship, the locus of ethical teaching, the unique example of service and sacrifice as demonstrated by his life and death, and the hermeneutic by which Scripture is to be interpreted. Gathering around Jesus in this manner as a community neither diminishes nor negates personal experiences of salvation, or personal insights into Scripture. However, gathering around Jesus with others can act as a hermeneutical corrective to personal faith experiences as individuals validate their experiences with the community.

Finally, the phrase "sent by him into the world" indicates that this community gathered around Jesus is also commanded by him to "go into all the world." The church will need to understand itself as "missional," rather than as just a congregation which supports denominational missions. A church which supports mission work can do so with relative indifference to its own community by sending funds to other places where missions activities are taking place. The missional church, however, is sent into the world. The difference in the two has tremendous implications for developing a ministry of reconciliation versus just contributing to a denominational missions program.

Secondly, Chatham Baptist Church can reimagine "church freedom," not as that which isolates it from other groups, but as a principle which frees it to collaborate with others without compromising its own core convictions. In its history, collaboration with others for the greater good of the community has resulted in Chatham Baptist Church founding Hargrave Military Academy, Samuel Harris Baptist Church, the Community Center, and the local Boys and Girls Club. In the past, rigid doctrinal positions have been instrumental in the SBC's decisions not to join the World Council of Churches, and to withdraw fellowship from the Baptist World Alliance. However, a more positive understanding of local church autonomy, coupled with its own history, could lead Chatham Baptist Church to work with local agencies, groups, and individuals to craft a ministry of reconciliation in the community without compromising its own practices or beliefs.

Third, "Bible freedom" could come to mean that Chatham Baptist Church reads Scripture in community with Jesus as the guiding hermeneutical principle. In fact, the *Baptist Faith and Message* of 1963 states in its section on "The Scriptures" that "the criterion by which the Bible is to be interpreted is Jesus Christ."[344] This phrase was changed in the *Baptist Faith and Message* of 2000 to read, "All Scripture is a testimony to Christ, who is Himself the focus of divine revelation." This change to the *Baptist Faith and Message* removed Jesus as the hermeneutical center. Embracing Jesus as the first hermeneutical principle of biblical interpretation would be simply an affirmation of the position the church already holds. The implications of this principle are that Chatham Baptist Church lives in primary obedience to the life, teaching, and example of Jesus Christ as reflected in the Bible. This obedience includes Christ's commands to love God, to forgive others, and to practice the kind of reconciling love found in the parables of the good Samaritan and the prodigal son.

Fourth, rather than "religious freedom" meaning either the privilege to worship without interference, or accommodation to the politics of the American right, Chatham Baptist Church might exercise its "religious freedom" to bear witness to the power of reconciliation before both government and society. By intentionally addressing racial barriers and discrimination, by advocating for the poor and disenfranchised, and by demonstrating its love for neighbor in practical ways, Chatham Baptist Church could critique barriers to reconciliation and model acts of reconciliation in its community. John Howard Yoder's book, *Body Politics*, provides theological interpretation for Chatham Baptist Church to understand its current practices as having the potential to provide theological witness to secular and civil entities.

Finally, rather than the church's mission being denominational "missions" programs, Chatham Baptist Church could embrace a wider ministry of reconciliation to God and others including individuals and groups, others outside the church membership, and God's created world. Based on the history of church and community, racial reconciliation still needs to be addressed in the Chatham, Pittsylvania County, and Danville communities. If it does so, Chatham Baptist Church might be able to say with the Apostle Paul, "All this is from God, who reconciled us to himself through Christ and gave us the ministry of reconciliation" (2 Corinthians 5:18).

# CHAPTER 5

# THEOLOGICAL AND THEORETICAL FOUNDATIONS OF RECONCILIATION

The concept of reconciliation is grounded in theology, and informed by the theories of various practices, perspectives, and academic disciplines, each of which contributes to a comprehensive understanding of reconciliation. Accordingly, this chapter is divided into six subsections, each dealing with one facet of the theory and practice of reconciliation.

In the first section, the biblical material concerning reconciliation will be examined to lay an appropriate foundation. The second section will explore the dynamics involved in reconciliation and will shed light on the actions which contribute to reconciliation. These include repentance and apology; forgiveness; judgment and justice; restitution and reparation; memory and narrative; and superordinate goal, also known as "the common good."

In the third section, selected parameters of reconciliation will be examined. These include ethnicity, class, religion, and relationships between individuals, groups, and nations. The fourth part of the chapter looks at reconciliation from the perspective of academic disciplines. Various studies offer their unique perspectives on reconciliation, such as forgiveness studies in psychology, race and ethnicity studies in sociology, and peace building studies. In the fifth part of the chapter, theology provides primary grounding for a ministry of reconciliation. Insights into the role of the community of the Spirit, empathy as prerequisite to reconciliation, reconciling practices, and reconciliation as the Church's signature ministry to the world will be examined. Finally, in the sixth part of the chapter the worshipping community will be identified as the locus of reconciliation work. The biblical narratives of Old and New Testaments, the historical account of the "cure of souls," and Dietrich Bonhoeffer's *Sanctorum Communio* will contribute to establishing the worshipping community as the central location of a ministry of reconciliation.

## The Biblical Material on Reconciliation

The Bible offers a rich resource on the subject of forgiveness and reconciliation. "It is fundamental to the biblical story that human beings exist in enmity, are alienated from God and from one another, and that Yahweh, the God of Israel, wills to overcome this enmity," write Gregory Baum and Howard Wells in their book, *The Reconciliation of Peoples* by.[345] While the Bible speaks of reconciliation between individuals and groups, the restoration of those relationships is predicated on God having provided through Christ the "means of reconciliation."[346]

In the Old Testament, instances of human estrangement from God and others are found frequently. In Genesis 3, the story of Adam and Eve is the paradigm of humankind's disobedience and estrangement from God. However, even as God casts Adam and Eve out of the Garden of Eden, God acts in their best interest by clothing them and prohibiting them from eating of the tree of life. This concern for disobedient humanity, which promises hope for reconciliation, recurs in the Old Testament.[347]

Another imperfect story of estrangement and reconciliation is King David's sin with Bathsheba (2 Samuel 11:1-5), and his subsequent attempt to cover it up by having Bathsheba's husband killed (2 Samuel 11:6-27). Nathan confronts David with his sin, proclaiming, "You are the man!" (2 Samuel 12:7). David acknowledges his sin, then waits contritely for the cycle of estrangement, forgiveness, and reconciliation to be completed (2 Samuel 12:11-25).

Those Old Testament stories are specific, yet imperfect examples of reconciliation. However, in his book, *Deep Memory,*

*Exuberant Hope*, Walter Brueggemann suggests that the Babylonian exile might provide the most complete narrative of estrangement and reconciliation in the Old Testament.[348] Brueggemann characterizes those who are estranged from God in exile as "dislocated folk."[349] Further, he suggests the experience of Jews in the Babylonian exile was a four-part process which moves from lament to hope. First, exiles avoided denial and lamented their situation with "*honesty, sadness, rage, anger, and loss.*"[350] Second, exiles reclaimed that which was lost, refusing to accept a "world thin and empty, without God."[351] Third, "the sounding of a voice of imaginative, neighborly transformation [is] focused on needy neighbors" and determines to do what is necessary to make relationships right. Finally, a new vision of the future, which Brueggemann calls "cadences of *new social possibility*," is "rooted in the truth of God's good news."[352]

While reconciliation is inferred in many Old Testament accounts, there are explicit instructions about reconciliation in the New Testament. Jesus' teaching makes forgiveness of others integral to praying The Lord's Prayer (Matthew 6:9-15), illustrating the connection between God's forgiveness and ours. However, the "Rule of Christ" in Matthew 18:15-18 contains the most specific instruction on how the faith community should handle incidents of offense and estrangement:

> If your brother or sister sins, go and point out their fault, just between the two of you. If they listen to you, you have won them over. But if they will not listen, take one or two others along, so that "every matter may be established by the testimony of two or three witnesses." If they still refuse to listen, tell it to the church; and if they refuse to listen even to the church, treat them as you would a pagan or a tax collector. Truly I tell you, whatever you bind on earth will be bound in heaven, and whatever you loose on earth will be loosed in heaven.

Yoder contends that when church members pursue reconciliation in this four-step process, their action is concurrent with "the activity of God."[353]

Following the teaching of Jesus, Paul lists forgiving among

the virtues of those in Christian community. In Colossians 3:13, Paul writes, "Bear with one another and, if anyone has a complaint against another, forgive each other; just as the Lord has forgiven you, so you also must forgive." In Ephesians 4:31-32, the apostle Paul exhorts, "Put away from you all bitterness and wrath and anger and wrangling and slander, together with all malice, and be kind to one another, tenderhearted, forgiving one another, as God in Christ has forgiven you." These passages include virtues which are related to those Jesus teaches in the Beatitudes (Matthew 5:3-11). These virtues, write Glen Stassen and David Gushee in their book, *Kingdom Ethics*, "are not merely an arbitrary selection; they are the heart of biblical virtues. They picture what it means to be a follower of Jesus."[354]

In summary, the biblical material dealing explicitly with forgiveness and reconciliation highlights several aspects. The overarching theme of the Old Testament is characterized by the exile, lament, reorientation, and hope surrounding the Babylonian exile. In the New Testament, Jesus recognized that among his followers there might be occasions of offense between them. He indicated that when those occurred, a process of engagement and forgiveness should follow. Moreover, expressions of forgiveness are expected of Jesus' followers because God in Christ has forgiven them. Finally, the practice of forgiveness and reconciliation demonstrates mercy and serves to maintain the unity of the New Testament faith community.[355]

## Dynamics Contributing to Reconciliation

The dynamics contributing to reconciliation are the specific actions engaged in by either the offender or the offended, or both, in order to restore their relationship. The first set of dynamics, repentance and apology, often is viewed as prerequisite to reconciliation.[356] Augsburger notes that "a full and sincere apology acknowledges the fact of the wrongdoing, accepts ultimate responsibility, expresses sincere sorrow and regret, and promises not to repeat the offense."[357] Apology can be made by one individual to another, by an individual to a group, by a group to an individual, or by one group to another group.[358] An example of group-to-group apology occurred in 1995 when the Southern Baptist Convention apologized for its defense of slavery in 1845, asking African-Americans for their forgiveness.[359] In summary, Augsburger sees repentance and apology as foundational to forgiveness and reconciliation. He writes, "As risks increase and trust unfolds, an appreciation of the other's perspective, the other's point of view, the other's sincerity in apology, and the authenticity of the repentance finally grows to the point where a respect for the other as genuine is achieved and both recognize that forgiveness has occurred."[360]

A second dynamic involved in the process of reconciliation is forgiveness. Augsburger describes forgiveness as "the mutual recognition that repentance is genuine and right relationships have been restored or achieved."[361] Augsburger's inclusion of both repentance and reconciliation as part of forgiveness focuses on the offended and the offender, and encompasses the "radical understanding of the forgiving community." [362] Echoing Augsburger's focus on a forgiving community, Gregory Jones suggests that forgiveness is a craft "that Christians are called to learn from one another."[363] In Christian community, forgiveness is expressed "through specific habits and practices that seek to remember the past truthfully, to repair the brokenness, to heal divisions, and to reconcile new relationships."[364] Even though Augsburger sees reconciliation as the indicator that genuine forgiveness has occurred, he also allows for a continuum of forgiveness experiences, ranging from unilateral forgiveness to mutual forgiveness. The goal, however, of the forgiveness spoken of in Matthew 18:15 remains "regaining the brother," according to Augsburger.[365]

The often conjoined elements of judgment and justice comprise a third dynamic in the process of reconciliation. In *The Shape of Practical Theology*, Ray Anderson contends that judgment is the verdict rendered by moral community on an offense. Following judgment, punishment is the appropriate consequence. When judgment is rendered and punishment executed, "justice has been rendered through moral judgment." However, despite the appropriateness of punishment, forgiveness can intervene as an alternative response after "moral judgment has been rendered and supported." According to Anderson, "Forgiveness does not excuse wrongdoing or bypass judgment; it only releases the offender from punishment." Anderson makes the connection from judgment to reconciliation when he states, "Forgiving is the costly grace of releasing one who is truly guilty from the consequences of the offense, all for the sake of and with the hope of reconciliation."[366]

A fourth dynamic that can help facilitate reconciliation is restitution or reparation. Augsburger defines restitution negatively and positively: "Restitution is not a repayment to avoid retaliation (anxiety) or return of equivalent value to earn acceptance (shame); it is the reestablishing of mutual justice. . . . It is the creative, responsive work of seeking justice between wrongdoer and wronged."[367] Restitution and reparation belong to actions intended to make amends. Margaret Urban Walker, in her book, *Moral Repair*, defines amends as "taking reparative action, but only action that issues from an acceptance of responsibility for *wrong*, and that embodies the will to set right something for which amends are *owed*."[368] Reparation or restitution can be an integral part of the reconciliation process.

Another cluster of dynamics involved in reconciliation is memory, narrative, and acknowledgement. Perhaps the classic example of the preservation of memory lies in the writing of Elie Wiesel. In the preface to his first book about the Holocaust titled, *Night*, Wiesel explains his reason for writing: "For the survivor who chooses to testify, it is clear: his duty is to bear witness for the dead *and* the living. He has no right to deprive future generations of a past that belongs to our collective memory. To forget would be not only dangerous but offensive; to forget the dead would be akin to killing them a second time."[369] Memory functions as a memorial to the event and those victimized by it.

However, telling the story to preserve it for future generations is not enough. Participants in reconciliation processes need to tell their stories and have them acknowledged so that healing may take place. In his book, *Justpeace Ethics*, Jarem Sawatsky contends that both victims and offenders need the space created by these narratives to "give voice to our story and to hear the other person."[370] The ability to name the injury is part of an "honest conversation about the past." When a "communal awareness is created about the truth of historical wounds, it can foster a host of official and unofficial initiatives for healing," writes Brian Cox in *Faith-Based Reconciliation*.[371]

A notable example of memory, narrative, and acknowledgement as a reconciliation dynamic is the work of the Truth and Reconciliation Commission (hereafter, TRC) in South Africa. The TRC was co-chaired by Anglican Archbishop Desmond Tutu. In his book, *No Future without Forgiveness*, Tutu describes the significance of the TRC's work:

> It was pointed out that we none of us possess a kind of fiat by which we can say, "Let bygones be bygones" and, hey presto, they then become bygones. Our common experience in fact is the opposite—that the past, far from disappearing or lying down and being quiet, has an embarrassing and persistent way of returning and haunting us unless it has in fact been dealt with adequately. Unless we look the beast in the eye we find it has an uncanny habit of returning to hold us hostage."[372]

In summary, memory, narrative, and acknowledgement play a substantial role in the reconciliation process. This cluster of dynamics "has been and may be the preconditions of genuine reconciliation," writes Stassen in *Just Peacemaking*.[373] When victims and offenders hear and are heard, when narratives are agreed upon, when wrongs are acknowledged, and apology and repentance accompany them, then serious groundwork has been laid for accomplishing reconciliation.

Finally, a sixth dynamic involved in reconciliation is a superordinate goal, that is, a quest for the common good.[374] In his book, *Reconciliation: Restoring Justice*, John W. de Gruchy describes the reconciliation South Africa sought as "a process in which there is a mutual attempt to heal and overcome enmities, build trust and relationships, and develop a shared commitment to the common good."[375]

An example of a superordinate goal in the reconciliation process lies in Virginia's history during the desegregation of public schools in the late 1950s. Led by Senator Harry Byrd, Virginia embarked on a course of "massive resistance" to the United States Supreme Court ruling in *Brown v. Board of Education*. For five years Virginia actively opposed school desegregation. However in 1959, after several unfavorable court rulings, and spurred by White "middle-class parents," the governor of Virginia led the state legislature to repeal its massive resistance legislation. In *The Moderates' Dilemma*, Matthew Lassiter and Andrew Lewis describe the convergence of both Black and White moderate voices in the process: "The broad-based African-American challenge to racial inequality and the defensive revolt of the [White] center against massive resistance heralded substantial political and educational gains in Virginia."[376] In Virginia's case, Blacks and moderate Whites together achieved the superordinate goal of re-opening Virginia's public schools.

In summary, the six dynamics contributing to reconciliation examined in this section include repentance and apology; forgiveness; judgment and justice; restitution and reparation; memory, narrative, and acknowledgement; and the superordinate goal, or common good. These dynamics may not all be present in each reconciliation experience, but some will. In seeking to practice a ministry of reconciliation, churches can become skilled at understanding and employing these dynamics as contributing elements in the reconciling process.

## Parameters of Reconciliation Work

In their book, *Reconciliation in Divided Societies: Finding Common Ground*, authors Erin Daly and Jeremy Sarkin sketch the parameters of reconciliation:

> Generally speaking, reconciliation describes coming together; it is the antithesis of falling or growing apart. Reconciliation has a normative—almost a moral—aspect as well. It is the coming together (or re-coming together) of things that *should* be together. Unlike its less common relative, conciliation, reconciliation connotes the coming together of things that once were united but have been torn asunder—a return to or recreation of the *status quo ante*, where real or imagined.[377]

In other words, the parameters of reconciliation are defined by that which has been sundered. As a result, the authors conclude, "The appeal of reconciliation is broad because its promise is virtually infinite."[378] However, for the limited purposes of this book, the focus will be on those commonly occurring rifts in society caused by ethnic strife, class conflicts, and religious antagonism.

# THE RECONCILING COMMUNITY

The first parameter of reconciliation work is conflict over ethnicity and race. Mark Noll writes in his book, *God and Race in American Politics*, "The Civil War solved the religion and slavery problem, but it did not solve the religion and race problem."[379] Miguel De La Torre offers corroborating insight to Noll's observation:

> All too often reconciliation is spiritualized. People from different races and ethnicities are envisioned holding hands and singing together a song such as "Kumbaya, my Lord, Kumbaya." . . . The reality is that once the [Promise Keepers] rally was over, the white men returned to their predominantly white neighborhoods and reported their successes in racial reconciliation to their predominantly white churches.[380]

Clearly, for De La Torre, racial reconciliation is at best a work unfinished, and at worst a sham display of sentimentality. Consequently, ethnic and racial conflict provides a continuing opportunity for authentic reconciliation work.

Closely related to ethnicity and race, class and caste issues form another parameter within which reconciliation work can be attempted. In Chapter 1, Sherrow Pinder's asserted that "class is substituted for race" often in American culture because "America's class system is distinctively racialized."[381] Class divisions based on economics, education, and status are significant factors in the community context of Chatham Baptist Church. In his book, *The Moral Imagination*, John Paul Lederach notes the differences in status between the African Dagomba and Konkomba tribes based on the fact that one had a chief and the other did not. This status differential led to hostility and animosity between the two tribes.[382] In short, the class to which a person or group belongs, whether in Virginia or Africa, can foster estrangement, hurt, or exclusion which needs reconciliation.

Another parameter is religious conflict. Whether Christian, Islamist, or belonging to another sect, religious fundamentalists are "fervently counteractive, often militant in their reaction" to those persons, practices, or governments considered threats to their heritage and belief system.[383] However, religion marks not just a

81

parameter of possible conflict, but also an arena in which alienation and reconciliation can be addressed. In the first chapter of *Religion and Peacebuilding*, contributors David Little and Scott Appleby sum up religion's contradictory stances with this description: "Indeed, one of our central themes in what follows is 'the ambivalence of the sacred'—the ability of religion to promote what might be called militancy on behalf of the other, as well as militancy aimed against the other. Religion promotes both intolerance and hatred, that is, as well as tolerance of the strongest type—the willingness to live with, explore, and honor difference."[384] In summary, religion potentially can be an arena of conflict or reconciliation.

Finally, relationships form a broad parameter for reconciliation work. As noted with a previous look at apology, reconciliation can take place between individuals, groups, and nations. Reconciliation work can be personal, political, psychological, religious, or combinations of some or all of these disciplines. From disputes between marriage partners to full-scale conflicts between nations, reconciliation work is done within the context of human relationships. Of course, Christian theology grounds reconciliation between persons, groups, and nations in the reconciling work of God in Christ, as has been noted previously. A church like Chatham Baptist Church may think that its ministry of reconciliation will be confined to interpersonal reconciliation, or at most, reconciliation between groups of people. However, Daly and Sarkin contend that reconciliation work is not only multi-faceted, but it is multi-layered as well. Writing about both large-scale conflict and reconciliation, Daly and Sarkin recognize that individual reconciliation must also take place within wider attempts at reconciliation. They state,

> "Any resolution of a political conflict must therefore incorporate the role of the people and address their relationship to one another. This in turn has drawn attention to the psychological needs of individuals who are recovering from trauma. . . . Individual healing then, is seen as having a public dimension."[385]

While churches like Chatham Baptist Church may not sit at the table of international peace building efforts, churches are uniquely positioned within communities to deal with at least some of the layers of complexity involved in reconciliation, particularly in the area of personal and community relationships.

## Perspectives on Reconciliation Work

Reconciliation work can be approached also through the perspectives of multiple academic disciplines. Certain disciplines offer unique insights into the theory and practice of reconciliation, including forgiveness studies in psychology, race and ethnic studies in sociology, and peace and justice studies. A brief review of each perspective and its potential contribution to a local church ministry of reconciliation will be offered.

The first perspective considered is forgiveness studies in the discipline of psychology. In *Helping Clients Forgive*, psychologists Robert Enright and Richard Fitzgibbons offer this definition of forgiveness:

> People, upon rationally determining that they have been unfairly treated, forgive when they willfully abandon resentment and related responses (to which they have a right), and endeavor to respond to the wrongdoer based on the moral principle of beneficence, which may include compassion, unconditional worth, generosity, and moral love (to which the wrongdoer, by nature of the hurtful act or acts, has no right).[386]

Enright and Fitzgibbons advocate phases in the forgiveness process which include uncovering the offense, deciding to forgive the offender, working at understanding and feeling empathy for the offender, and deepening one's insights into forgiveness in general.[387] In similar fashion Everett Worthington, in his book, *Dimensions of Forgiveness*, advocates a five-step plan of forgiveness.[388]

Interestingly, psychology's approach to forgiveness separates forgiveness from reconciliation. Forgiveness may occur intra-personally and unilaterally, without the necessity of the offended reconciling with their offender. Enright and Fitzgibbons suggest that the fear of returning to a hurtful relationship is an impediment to forgiveness work, and therefore reconciliation should be separated from forgiveness.[389]

Psychology's model of forgiveness focuses on the individual forgiver, and the benefits of forgiveness experienced in terms of improved emotional health.[390] While this positive effect is beneficial, this approach alone is not adequate as the basis for a church ministry of reconciliation because it is less concerned with the restoration of community than it is with the benefits that accrue to the forgiver. This client-centered approach neglects the clear intent of the Rule of Christ, which is to have "won your brother over" (Matthew 18:15).

Having noted psychology's approach to forgiveness that focuses on the individual, attention now turns to sociology's model for dealing with race and ethnicity issues. Race is generally agreed to be a social construct, and is defined by Vincent Parillo in *Understanding Race and Ethnic Relations* in this manner: "Race is a categorization in which a large number of people sharing visible biological characteristics regard themselves or are regarded by others as a single group on that basis."[391] Parillo distinguishes race from ethnicity by defining an ethnic group to include the three elements of race, religion, and national origin.[392]

Other sociologists, such as Douglas S. Massey, write about the problems encountered by minorities in the United States. Massey's book, *Categorically Unequal: The American Stratification System*, deals with the mechanism of social stratification in the United States: "Stratification refers to the unequal distribution of people across social categories that are characterized by differential access to scarce resources. The resources may be material, such as income and wealth; they may be symbolic, such as prestige and social standing; or they may be emotional, such as love affection, and, of course, sex."[393]

Eduardo Bonilla-Silva writes about "color-blind racism" in his book, *Racism without Racists: Color-Blind Racism and Racial Inequality in Contemporary America*. The thrust of Bonilla-Silva's book is that "[for] most whites racism is prejudice, [while] for most people of color racism is systemic or institutionalized."[394] Bonilla-Silva argues that Whites have learned the artifice of "smiling face" discrimination, while perpetuating the institutional racism that continues to exist in American culture.[395]

Finally, the discipline of peace building and its related

emphases of restorative justice and conflict transformation also offer opportunities to explore reconciliation. A veteran peace builder and academic, John Paul Lederach, suggests that reconciliation is "the place where Truth and Mercy, Justice and Peace meet."[396] Sustainable reconciliation, according to Lederach, is a "reconciliation that will endure because it is sustained by a society-wide network of relationships and mechanisms that promote justice and address the root causes of enmity before they can regenerate destabilizing tensions."[397]

Reconciliation addresses three specific "paradoxes" according to Lederach. First, "reconciliation promotes an encounter between the open expression of a painful past, on the one hand, and the search for the articulation of a long-term interdependent future, on the other hand."[398] Second, reconciliation offers space to hear what has happened in the past, and for "letting go" in favor of renewed relationships. Third, reconciliation addresses both justice and peace, "when redressing the wrong is held together with the envisioning of a common, connected future."[399] Peace building, restorative justice, and conflict transformation seek renewed relationships, truth-telling about the past, reparations and restitution as appropriate, conversations in which each can be heard and acknowledged, and repentance and apology where needed.

## The Primacy of Theology for the Christian Ministry of Reconciliation

Having surveyed the dynamics, parameters, and perspectives of reconciliation work, the focus turns back to the primacy of theology for the Christian ministry of reconciliation. Norman Kraus, in his book, *The Community of the Spirit*, calls the community constituted by the Spirit of God at Pentecost, a "community of witness."[400] This community, known as the Church, was not to begin its mission until "the Father had completed the formation of the new body through which the Christ would expand his presence and ministry."[401] This "new disciple community" was completed with the "gift of the Spirit at Pentecost."[402] Individuals who are formed into this new community are "persons-in-covenant-community," and as such they find their identity and express the image of God in relationship with God and others.[403] Just as the goal of God's covenant with Adam was to create a "community of shalom," so this new community is involved in "an outward movement of forgiveness and reconciliation, of personal interdependence and sharing of God's purpose for the cosmos."[404] In other words, Kraus further explains: "The 'kingdom of God' which Jesus promoted is a community, or *koinonia*, of individuals in submission to the authority of God's covenant of 'life and peace' (Malachi 2:5)."[405] As such, this community is the "authentic continuation of the ministry of Jesus."[406] Jesus explicitly authorizes this community to do as he did, to forgive sins, and "thus free people from their shame, fear, and guilt," writes Kraus.[407] He continues, "The keys are thus for the purpose of opening doors to reconciliation and healing."[408] William Klassen, in his book, *The Forgiving Community*, notes, "Although God is the ultimate source of forgiveness, and although Christ is the primary agent who achieved forgiveness for man, it is still the church, the empirical church living in history, that serves as God's main instrument in mediating forgiveness."[409]

However, the Church is not only to extend forgiveness, and by implication reconciliation, but the Church is to empathetically incarnate the concept of forgiveness and reconciliation. Glen Harold Stassen writes of incarnational ministry as empathy in his book, *A Thicker Jesus: Incarnational Discipleship in a Secular Age*: "As God entered history incarnationally in Jesus, and as Jesus entered compassionately into the midst of the lives of outcasts, so we are called to enter incarnationally into the lives of others. . . . Thus 'incarnational' discipleship also has the meaning of 'empathetically entering into the pain of others and taking personal responsibility for acting on their behalf.'"[410]

Augsburger offers the idea of "presence" as a vision of incarnational discipleship. "*Presence* is the quality of *being there* for and with another. It is being oneself for someone else."[411] He continues, "This *presence* becomes a virtue as it expresses the narrative of a community that acts in the tradition of incarnation, of embodiment of neighbor-love, of willing service to human need. . . . *Forgiveness* is the quality of being with another in spite of the injury done or alienation mutually experienced."[412] Augsburger focuses on empathy as necessary to forgiveness and reconciliation with someone who is "other." He writes, "Seeing our common experience, frailty, and failures evokes compassion; empathizing with what is foreign, fearsome, even repugnant invites us to engage and be engaged by what we do not perceive within ourselves because of its absence or our lack of insight."[413]

Thus far it has been noted that theologically, the community of the Spirit living empathetically as the incarnation of God's love and forgiveness is the theological basis for a ministry of reconciliation. Moreover, this community of the Spirit, called the Church, also has inherent practices that can facilitate reconciliation. In his book, *Reconciliation: Mission and Ministry in a Changing Social Order*, Robert J. Schreiter observes practices of communities of the Spirit that bear witness to reconciliation. The first of these is an "attitude of listening and waiting." Those victimized by violence, suffering, and estrangement need time to tell their stories over and again. This retelling of personal stories allows the narrator to "tame its savage power" and in time to be able to "construct a new narrative of truth" without being overwhelmed by the violence of his or her experience. Waiting serves a similar function as patient listening. Neither listening nor waiting is passive; rather, both are active practices that Schreiter contends move participants "out of illusion—the narrative of the lie—into reality—the narrative of the truth."[414]

The second practice is "attention and compassion." Schreiter uses "attention" in the sense of *attending to* a task. He writes, "Just as any spirituality cannot hope to grow without turning its attention constantly to God, so too attention to healing of painful memories is of the essence in the ministry of reconciliation." Compassion (or empathy), the companion to attention, allows reconcilers to "feel or suffer with" others.[415]

Finally, the third practice or characteristic is to adopt a "post-exilic stance." Drawing from the experience of the Babylonian exile in the Hebrew Scriptures, this "post-exilic stance" recognizes that "a new society will have to be constructed on the ruins of the old society."[416] This requires "a *deutoronomos*, a second law" and "a chastened outlook to the returnees," according to Schreiter.[417] The post-exile narrative of estrangement and return provides rich soil which can sustain a "spirituality of reconciliation."[418]

## The Worshipping Community as Locus of Reconciliation

The final concern of this chapter in addressing the theological and theoretical aspects of a ministry of reconciliation is where to situate such a ministry. Some might suggest the topic of reconciliation is suitable for discussion in a Christian education setting. Others might see a ministry of reconciliation as belonging to the missions or outreach program of a church. However, the scope of this book is to present a strategy for the congregation of Chatham Baptist Church to reimagine itself as a missional community of reconciliation by learning about reconciliation during worship, which means the faith community gathered for worship is the intentional locus from which the congregation learns and reflects on reconciliation as a its core ministry to the world.

In *A Theological Introduction to the Old Testament*, Bruce C. Birch, Walter Brueggemann, Terence E. Fretheim, and David L. Petersen contend that worship sprang from the law of God for Israel, with a primary concern about creation. They explain that worship became the "means by which the people of God can (a) take on the characteristics of that new creation in their own life and (b) participate in the divine efforts to reclaim creation."[419] The tabernacle, the authors contend, is a "microcosm of creation, God's intended world order writ small in Israel, a beginning in God's mission to bring creation to where it is perfectly reflective of the divine will."[420] Furthermore, worship may have been local, but "its concerns and effects are cosmic," according to the authors. In other words, worship in Old Testament Israel was "for the sake of the world . . . a God-given way for the people of God to participate in the recreation of a new world."[421]

N. T. Wright, in his book, *The New Testament and the People of God*, suggests that in early Christian churches, "mission and sacrament both came into focus at the very centre of the church's life, that is, its worship."[422] Wright connects worship with "a clear ethical code," which assumed that Christians would behave differently from their pagan neighbors. This code, Wright contends, was "astonishing in a world where trust and affection were normally confined to family and friends—they cared for one another across the barriers formed by normal culture."[423] In both Old Testament worship and the worship of the early Church, these features of a community gathered for the life of the world demonstrate that worship is central in the life and mission the people of God. It is that same theological rationale that locates reconciliation first and foremost in the community of faith gathered for worship.

However, the history of the "cure of souls" also provides an additional rationale for situating reconciliation in worship. William Willimon, in his book, *Worship As Pastoral Care*, recognizes Charles Jaeckle and William Clebsch who "delineated four historic functions of pastoral care: healing, sustaining, guiding, and reconciling."[424] Furthermore, pastoral care was expressed first in the early Church in worship through the Eucharist. As the Church matured and suffered persecution, "reconciliation of lapsed souls into the life of the church through acts of penance and contrition became a central focus of the care of souls."[425] However, with the Reformation of the sixteenth century, "the sacraments in particular and public worship in general lost their place as chief loci of pastoral care in the churches that emerged from the Reformation."[426] Willimon explains the effect of this shift: "In an earlier time, a pastor caring for his flock, engaging in activities related to the cure of souls meant, in great part, leading them in worship. . . . Reconciling, pastoral care for the reestablishment of broken relationships among people and between people and God, traditionally meant those ritualized acts of forgiveness, confession, penance, and absolution."[427] In light of the historic shift of pastoral care functions, including reconciliation, from acts of worship to transactions between individuals, it is incumbent that reconciliation again be located in worship itself.

Finally, the work of Dietrich Bonhoeffer offers a third rationale for locating reconciliation primarily in the worship experience. In his magnum opus, *Sanctorum Communio: A Theological Study of the Sociology of the Church*, Bonhoeffer provides a theological basis for the gathering of the church in worship: "*The assembly embodies God's will to use the social connections between human beings to extend God's rule. The objective spirit of the church-community actualizes this will of God by establishing regular worship. Assembling for worship belongs to the essence of the church-community*" [Bonhoeffer's italics].[428] Bonhoeffer then explains the effect this assembly for worship has, and how the assembly itself reflects reconciliation between God and others:

As such it becomes a serious concrete community, for it includes Jew and Greek, slave and free. As such it stands not only in the world, but against the world as the power of an objective spirit that has a moral will and courageous determination. The public assembly is thus both God's will and act of the church-community, and therefore not only something that takes place between God and the church-community, but also something between the church-community and the world.[429]

In summary, a local church's ministry of reconciliation must have as its locus the worship experience of the gathered faith community. From the Old Testament worship of the nation of Israel, to the early Church, to the contemporary Church of Bonhoeffer's day and beyond, worship is the uniting experience in which "the church-community pledges itself to God, according to God's will; and here God pledges to be present within the church-community."[430] Bonhoeffer explains that this "shows that church is something 'visible,' a community of human beings consisting of body and soul; it is not a community of common convictions or based on kindred spirits, but a community of love made up of real human beings."[431]

## Conclusion

In conclusion, Chapter 5 has examined the unique insights and approaches to reconciliation that theology, psychology, sociology, and peace building studies contribute. Working from the position that each discipline is important to the work of a church seeking to become a reconciling community, the dynamics, parameters, and perspectives of each discipline have been reviewed. The primacy of theology has been reiterated as the foundation for the practice of reconciliation drawn from multiple disciplines. Finally, the worshipping community has been shown to be the appropriate locus for a local church ministry of reconciliation. This chapter, then, provides the rationale for the strategy which will be presented in Chapters Six and Seven.

# CHAPTER 6

# CRAFTING A MISSIONAL COMMUNITY OF RECONCILIATION

This chapter brings together the theological implications, the content, the goals, and the leadership and participants in the strategy to re-image the church's ministry. Through a coordinated series of worship experiences, amplified by small group study, participants will read Scripture, hear sermons and stories, interact with presentations, and participate in decision-making to transform the congregation into a practitioner of reconciliation. Goals for the strategy are measurable, achievable, and reflect progressive steps in implementing the vision of transforming Chatham Baptist Church into a missional community of reconciliation.

### Theological Implications for a Reconciling Community

In Chapters 1 and 2, the contexts of community and church have been examined in order to understand the narratives that have shaped their experiences of estrangement and reconciliation. In Chapter 3, literature pertinent to the topic has been reviewed and evaluated as to each work's contribution to the subject of reconciliation in general, and to its specific application in the life and ministry of Chatham Baptist Church. In Chapter 4, Baptist ecclesiology has been described, critiqued, and reimagined in order to provide a more suitable milieu in which to implement and sustain a ministry of reconciliation. Finally, in Chapter 5, the theological and theoretical dimensions of reconciliation have been studied in order to ground this project in a firm theological footing, while informing it with the helpful insights from other academic disciplines.

The previous discussion now culminates in a strategy of a reconciliation ministry in and through Chatham Baptist Church. As such, theology again provides the ground of first contact as the theological implications for the church and its mission are considered. Those implications involve three activities, each revealing a facet of reconciliation that will become evident as Chatham Baptist Church reimagines itself as a missional community of reconciliation.

The first of these facets encompasses the church's witness to itself and the outside world. Yoder writes about the overall purpose of God in his book, *He Came Preaching Peace*: "According to the Bible, the purpose of God always has a social shape. The purpose of God is peace in real human shared experience."[432] Walter Brueggemann expands on the meaning of peace by defining it as "that persistent vision of joy, well-being, harmony, and prosperity" whose nuances include the concepts of "love, loyalty, truth, grace, salvation, justice, blessing, and righteousness."[433] The word used to gather up all of these concepts into one expression is the word *shalom*. According to Brueggemann, "*Shalom* is the substance of the biblical vision of one community embracing all creation."[434] However, *shalom*—peace—is not a static, realized destination, but an ever-challenging journey. Brueggemann observes that "the origin and destiny of God's people are to be on the road of *shalom*, which is to live out of joyous memories and toward greater anticipations."[435] He further adds that "*shalom* comes only to the inclusive, embracing community that excludes none."[436]

David Bosch, in *Transforming Mission*, contends that in Luke's Gospel and in the book of Acts, a component of Luke's model of mission was "preaching the good news of peace by Jesus Christ."[437] Bosch lists a total of eight parts to Luke's theology of mission, but he notes a critical significance about the preaching of peace: "Our missionary involvement may be very successful in other respects, but if we fail here, we stand guilty before the Lord of mission. Peacemaking, I therefore suggest, is a major ingredient of Luke's missionary paradigm."[438] In Luke 24:36-49, the resurrected Jesus appears to his disciples for the last time before his ascension into heaven. Jesus' words of greeting to the disciples to whom he appears are "Peace be with you." (Luke 24:36). After reassuring his disciples of his identity by inviting them to touch him, and by eating some broiled fish, he offered these words of explanation and instruction:

> He said to them, "This is what I told you while I was still with you: Everything must be fulfilled that is written about me in the Law of Moses, the Prophets and the Psalms." Then he opened their minds so they could understand the Scriptures. He told them, "This is what is written: The Christ will suffer and rise from the dead on the third day, and repentance and forgiveness of sins will be preached in his name to all nations, beginning at Jerusalem. You are witnesses of these things. (Luke 24:44-48)

Bosch explains what this means for the future of the disciple community and the Church itself: "It is dedicated to telling us not just how perplexed observers became Easter believers, but how uncomprehending eyewitnesses were made witnesses of the risen Christ, sharers of the messianic destiny, and spokespersons of the word of forgiveness in his name to all the nations."[439]

This idea of "witness" in the Gospel of Luke "becomes the appropriate term for mission" in the book of Acts, writes Bosch.[440] What was witnessed to was "the good news of the reign of God *is* Jesus Christ, incarnated, crucified and risen, and what he has accomplished."[441] However, the apostles themselves are not called to "accomplish anything, only to point to what God has done and is doing, to give testimony to what they have seen and heard and touched."[442]

A central theme in this witness of the apostles and the early Church is the theme of forgiveness and reconciliation. Yoder contends that "The Rule of Christ" in Matthew 18:15-18 continued to be a "procedure for concrete peacemaking, a pattern for practice and training in the acting out of the making of peace."[443] Yoder lists four significant implications of Matthew 18:15-18 for both the early Church and the Church today. First, "to bind and to loose" referred to a rabbinic practice, but "also the process of moral discernment. There is an intimate link between forgiving and making ethical decisions," according to Yoder.[444] Second, this passage is "strategically important" because the apostle Paul alludes to it in 1 Corinthians 6:1-8, when he urges Corinthian Christians to settle disputes among themselves rather than taking each other to secular courts. Third, during the Reformation Martin Luther and Martin Bucer apparently both used the term "rule of Christ" to refer to this passage. Furthermore, Anabaptists understood it to provide a "nonviolent Christian alternative to the sword," states, Yoder, when settling disputes. For Anabaptists, the "rule of Christ" became one of three "ordinances" they believed Christ commanded, the other two being the Lord's Supper and baptism. Fourth, Yoder points to the influence of this passage on contemporary disciplines of conflict resolution. He concludes by writing, "The world knows, even though the church hesitates to recognize it, that this pattern of peacemaking is both possible and indispensible."[445]

In addition to witness, a theology of reconciliation becomes a potential bridge from the past traditional ministry of Chatham Baptist Church to its future as a missional community. Roxburgh and Boren identify rather than define the term *missional church* using three criteria. They write, "Missional church is about an alternative imagination for being the church. It is about this transformation toward a church that is shaped by *mystery*, *memory*, and *mission*."[446] Roxburgh and Boren suggest that the component of *mystery* in the concept of missional church lies in "*being chosen by God to represent him for the sake of the world.*"[447] Just as the existence and mission of the nation of Israel cannot be satisfactorily explained by the personalities of Abraham or Moses, or even the human aspiration for freedom, so the existence of the Church cannot be explained by any means other than of God's choosing.[448] Roxburgh and Boren explain,

> Those called into the church did not join a voluntary society; they are called and chosen by God. They are called to be a sign, witness, and foretaste of God's coming kingdom. To participate in the missional journey is to embrace this mystery and allow this reality to overwhelm and supersede the pressing matters of being a successful church or growing the church, which seem to dominate our imaginations.[449]

In similar fashion, the idea of *memory* forms a second component in describing the missional church. Roxburgh and Boren note that Israel was shaped by "a very specific memory rooted in events and stories of God's actions to, for, and with Israel."[450] Events, and their memorialized rehearsal, such as the Passover, relive and celebrate the work of God in a specific place and time, but also vivify the present and offer hope for the future. The memorial meal in Christian worship called the Eucharist is an act of memory, recalling a past event, but one that also speaks to both present and future. However, memory also offers a narrative of contrast to the narrative of the dominant culture. This "alternative story" shapes the present, and forms the people of God into a community living in contrast to its surrounding culture. Roxburgh and Boren write, "Missional church is about a people of memory being continually formed in practices that shape us as an alternative story in our culture."[451]

Finally, Roxburgh and Boren declare that "mission is the outgrowth of mystery and memory." Unlike the traditional ministry of Chatham Baptist Church's past, mission is not a program of the church. Rather, mission is "what the church is through the mystery of its formation and memory of its calling. The church is God's missionary people. There is no participation in Christ without participation in God's mission in the world."[452] The mission of Chatham Baptist Church must be transformed from support for the denomination's missions programs into the heart of the church's purpose and practice.

The concept of the missional church based in mystery, memory, and mission can create a new imagination for the congregation of Chatham Baptist Church. This new imagination can build on the past experiences of the church in its concern for those in its community and world, but can also refocus the church in a new direction—becoming a reconciling community of faith for the life of the world. This bridge from the church's traditional past to its missional future will enable the church to realize a new role as a congregation called and sent by God into the world with the ministry of reconciliation.

Finally, the third theological implication for the congregation of Chatham Baptist Church builds on the idea of its becoming a missional church. As a missional community, the church will incarnate its own experience of reconciliation with God and each other, and extend that same reconciliation to its community and the world. Yoder has already been quoted as saying that "the people of God [are] called to be today what the world is called to be ultimately."[453] Roxburgh and Boren contend that the Church is called to be a "public *sign, witness,* and *foretaste*" of where God is inviting all of creation to be through the Holy Spirit.[454] Churches become sign, witness, and foretaste of God's kingdom by "developing habits," state Roxburgh and Boren, such as "practicing hospitality, learning to be present in the community, and inviting those in their neighborhoods to taste and see what it means to be shaped by Jesus."[455]

Part of being a sign, witness, and foretaste of God's new creation is the practice of reconciliation between persons and God, and between human beings with each other. This type of reconciliation leads to a community that lives and demonstrates the concept of *shalom*. When Jesus sent out the disciples in Matthew 10, he gave them the "authority to mediate 'peace,' that is God's salvation" (Matthew 10:11). He said, "Whatever town or village you enter, find out who in it is worthy, and stay there until you leave. As you enter the house, greet it. If the house is worthy, let your peace come upon it; but if it is not worthy, let your peace return to you." (Matthew 10:12-13). Jesus gives this same "authority to mediate peace" to the Church today. Likewise, just as the apostle Paul extended the hope of reconciliation to those in Corinth, so Chatham Baptist Church will extend that same reconciliation which leads to the *shalom* of God in like manner.

> All this is from God, who reconciled us to himself through Christ and gave us the ministry of reconciliation: that God was reconciling the world to himself in Christ, not counting people's sins against them. And he has committed to us the message of reconciliation. We are therefore Christ's ambassadors, as though God were making his appeal through us. We implore you on Christ's behalf: Be reconciled to God. (2 Corinthians 5:18-20)

### Criteria for a Preferred Future

In light of the theological implications of a ministry of reconciliation for Chatham Baptist Church, the criteria for evaluating a ministry of reconciliation must be explored. The question to be answered is: What will a ministry of reconciliation look like at Chatham Baptist Church? In other words, the church must define the result for which it is striving in order to know if it has been achieved. In similar fashion to the definition of forgiveness, the term *reconciliation* can be ambiguous and "means different things to different people, who use it at different times for different purposes," according to Mark DeYmaz, in his book, *Building a Healthy Multi-Ethnic Church: Mandate, Commitments, and Practices of a Diverse Congregation*.[456] The church DeYmaz founded, Mosaic in Little Rock, Arkansas, states in its statement of purpose, "Mosaic is not a church focused on racial reconciliation. Rather, we are focused on reconciling men and women to God through faith in Jesus Christ and on reconciling ourselves with the principles and practices of local churches as described in the New Testament."[457]

However, DeYmaz seems to contradict the church's purpose statement when he states his conviction that multicultural churches are biblically mandated: "And let me make one thing perfectly clear from the start: pursuit of the multi-ethnic local church is, in my view, not optional. It is biblically mandated for all who would aspire to lead a local congregation of faith."[458] Apparently, according to DeYmaz, congregations must be multicultural to be faithful congregations in the New Testament tradition. Of course, this addresses Dr. King's oft-quoted observation that eleven o'clock on Sunday morning is still "the most segregated hour" of the week.[459] However, multiculturalism is not "in and of itself . . . the answer to inequality and justice," according to Michael O. Emerson and Rodney M. Woo in their book, *People of the Dream: Multiracial Congregations in the United States*.[460] According to the authors, multiculturalism is the latest in a progression of "shifting visions" or "metaphors for U. S. race and ethnic relations."[461]

For Chatham Baptist Church, multiculturalism is a new experience. Only since the founding of the Boys and Girls Club of Chatham in 2005 has the church enjoyed consistent attendance and participation by African-Americans, and these have been predominantly children and teenagers. Clearly, while on the way to a more diverse congregation, a ministry of reconciliation must involve more than multiracial attendance at church events.

Based on the context of the church and community, the survey of the biblical and academic resources, the theological rationale, and the reimagining of church ecclesiology and mission, a broader range of criteria than multiculturalism should be considered. The preferred future for a ministry of reconciliation at Chatham Baptist Church should involve five criteria: continuity with the best of the church's past; discontinuity with the community's culture of prejudice and discrimination; mutual conversation and corporate confession; humility and trust regarding institutional power; and a shared cross-cultural commitment to work together to transform community institutions including churches, schools, civic clubs, criminal justice agencies, and local businesses. These criteria will give shape to a contextually sensitive, theologically grounded, missional approach to reconciliation in Chatham, Virginia and its surrounding area.

First, the church's ministry of reconciliation should give evidence of continuity with the best of its past history. As previously noted, both the church and the community value their past histories. Selected members of the congregation have participated in Appreciative Inquiry interviews conducted for this course of study. Participants reflected on the best of church leadership and accomplishments, and identified times when they felt most engaged and fulfilled in their church. Appreciative Inquiry focuses on the "positive core" of an organization's history, leadership, and future aspirations.[462] As such, it is an ideal technique to capture the best of Chatham Baptist Church's 155-year history and experience. Positive continuity with the church's past will help build a bridge to its missional future.

Secondly, although the church values the traditions and history of its past, it also must recognize and consciously acknowledge that its past also contained a prejudice and discrimination that was not faithful to the *missio Dei*, particularly in its attitude toward African-Americans. There must be a change, a discontinuity, from this aspect of the church's cultural past. In the book, *The Gospel in Black and White: Theological Resources for Racial Reconciliation*, Cheryl J. Sanders suggests that churches interested in racial reconciliation adopt an exilic identity. She writes, "A church with an exilic identity is an alternative community formed by a coherent set of values at odds with the surrounding culture."[463] This "surrounding culture" can also refer to a community's past actions and memory. Reinventing itself as an alternative community would be consistent with the church's newly imagined missional theology and praxis.

Third, a church ministry of reconciliation must engage in mutual conversation and corporate confession with groups with whom the church is seeking reconciliation. In his book, *The Next Evangelicalism: Freeing the Church from Western Cultural Captivity*, Soong-Chan Rah writes, "Corporate confession begins with awareness—the awareness of the reality of corporate sin and the racially oppressive history connected to that corporate sin."[464] However, before confession is rendered, the parties must have a conversation where all have a chance to speak without interruption, and for the purpose of opening a dialogue which leads to healing and transformation. Circle processes could provide a technique for such a dialogue, and will be explored later in the context of the pilot project itself.

Fourth, if the church is going to engage in a ministry of reconciliation, then it must approach that ministry with humility, and with the understanding that power is an issue. Power is defined by Emerson and Woo as "the capacity of some people or groups to produce intended and foreseen effects on others. The misuse of power is the use of power for one group against the wishes of another group."[465] Soong-Chan Rah observes, "Very few who have the power and privilege of white cultural captivity will be willing to yield that power in order to prepare for the next stage of the American church."[466] Even in so-called multicultural congregations, Emerson observed multiple examples of the misuse of power by the dominant group in music selection, religious art, paternalism, ignorance of other cultures, evaluation of history and heroes, race or the failure to acknowledge racial issues, assimilation, and more.[467] He notes,

> Misused power is the closest thing I observed to a nightmare in the multiracial congregations. Congregations that seemed able to reduce such problems had clear-cut standards that were institutionalized, such that the voices of all groups were included. Not having standards for such inclusiveness eventually led to the misuse of power that adversely affected

members of some groups more than members of other groups.⁴⁶⁸

Power-sharing and the majority's "willingness to submit to the spiritual authority of nonwhites" are seen as key points by Rah.⁴⁶⁹

Fifth and finally, a shared cross-cultural commitment to work together to transform community institutions including churches, schools, civic clubs, criminal justice agencies, and local businesses becomes the evidence of reconciliation at work, particularly in the area of racial reconciliation. Already noted is Bonilla-Silva's assertion: "Whereas for most whites racism is prejudice, for most people of color racism is systemic or institutionalized."⁴⁷⁰ This criterion is difficult because it moves beyond the realm of personal prejudice, which many Whites deny, and into the wider society and its institutions. Bonilla-Silva states, "Therein lies the secret of racial structures and racial inequality the world over. They exist because they benefit the members of the dominant race."⁴⁷¹ Previously noted in Chapter 1 was the failure of established White leaders in Chatham and Danville, Virginia to open space for leaders who are younger, female, or Black. The same might be noted of Chatham Baptist Church, which has no Black adult members.

On the denominational level, the Southern Baptist Convention, which has just elected its first African-American president,⁴⁷² has no African-Americans as directors of its myriad agencies or educational institutions. Southern Baptist African-American pastor Dwight McKissic asks, "How could the SBC not see that the platform is generally all White at the annual session? How could the SBC not see that all of her entity heads are White?"⁴⁷³ If Chatham Baptist Church, in a humble conversation with African-American leaders in the community, commits to working with them to change the power structure of institutions, then sustainable reconciliation will be possible. Such conversations would follow the pattern begun when the church initiated its role of hosting the Boys and Girls Club and constructing the Community Center. Given the contexts of both church and community, these five criteria address areas that need reconciling, and their presence will be evidence of reconciliation in process.

## Goals for Individual Transformation within the Strategy

In addition to the church being transformed by its transition to being a missional community of reconciliation, individual members within the congregation may also be changed in the process. Five goals for individual transformation during the implementation of the project include: affirming a biblical theology of church as a missional community, embracing the transforming power of reconciliation in relationships, empathizing with others as prerequisite to reconciliation practices, understanding the main themes of reconciliation across disciplines, and participating in designing and implementing a community reconciliation project.

As with the church congregation collectively, individual transformation should begin with a theological foundation. The first goal of the project is that individuals will affirm a biblical theology of church as a missional community. The core concept in defining the missional church is the *missio Dei*—the mission of God. Bosch explains how the theological understanding of the *missio Dei* has changed. He writes, "The classic doctrine on the *missio Dei* as God the Father sending the Son, and God the Father and the Son sending the Spirit was expanded to include yet another 'movement': Father, Son and Holy Spirit sending the church into the world."[474]

Lois Barrett, in Guder's *Missional Church*, identifies four elements involved in the sending of the Church into the world. First, Barrett suggests that the Church is "in, but not of, the world."[475] This means that while a missional church may "live in the context of the surrounding culture, engage with the culture, [it is not] controlled by the culture."[476] The church, Barrett contends, is called to be a community "not controlled by idolatrous powers, not conformed to the common sense of the surrounding culture, but shaping its life and ministry around Jesus Christ, his life, his death, and his resurrected power, and living now according to the pattern of the resurrected life of the age to come."[477] This is consistent with the proposal in Chapter 4, that the congregation might imagine itself as a faith community gathered around Jesus and sent by him into the world. Second, the missional church is a "holy nation among the nations."[478]

Barrett continues, "This new people is not a community in isolation from the world. It is, instead, a community engaged with the world in order to proclaim the mighty acts of the One who has called them out of darkness into God's marvelous light (1 Peter 2:9)."[479] As such, the church creates an alternative culture with its own vocabulary, economics, and alternative understanding of power.[480] Third, the missional church is inherently a community as mission, not just a community with a mission. The missional church is a "city set on a hill" and the "total life of the 'people sent' makes a difference to its apostolic witness. Furthermore, the church shares in the death and resurrection of Jesus through suffering and by sharing the eschatological vision of "God's rearranging things at the end of the age so that God's justice and God's peace prevail and so that the new community, the new Jerusalem, is fully established."[481] Finally, to embrace a missional theology of the Church means to continue the work of Jesus. The preaching, teaching, and healing ministry of Jesus, continued in and through the missional church, functions "to gather in people for the reign of God, and are the vocation of Jesus' disciples."[482] Barrett notes that "according to 2 Corinthians 5:18-20, that mission is to promote reconciliation with God and among peoples."[483]

In addition to affirming a biblical theology of the church as a missional community, participants in Chatham Baptist Church's reconciliation ministry will, secondly, embrace the transforming power of reconciliation in relationships. While the theoretical aspects of reconciliation have been explored, and are crucial to a comprehensive understanding of the many facets of reconciliation, the narratives of reconciliation offer the promise of capturing what Paul Lederach calls "the moral imagination."[484] Participants need to learn the mechanics of reconciling practices, but the theoretical also must be supplemented with the experiential—the true stories of the power of reconciliation in real life.

One such story from South Africa's struggle for forgiveness and reconciliation is the story of Nelson Mandela's example. Archbishop Desmond Tutu writes, "The miracle of South Africa's relatively peaceful transition from apartheid's repression to freedom of democracy was in large measure due to a decision to follow the path of reconciliation rather than retribution and revenge, to seek to forgive rather than to pay back in the same coin. God was so good to have given us a Nelson Mandela at this crucial moment in our history."[485] Archbishop Tutu then recalls the story of Mandela's election as the first president of the newly constituted South African democracy. After spending twenty-seven years in prison, Mandela might have been expected to emerge from that ordeal demanding "the blood of his tormentors."[486] Instead, however, President Mandela invited his former jailer to attend his inauguration as a "V.I.P. guest of the new president."[487] In addition, Mandela invited the former prosecutor at his trial, Dr. Percy Yutar, to lunch upon his inauguration. "This was how Nelson Mandela advanced the cause of reconciliation, not just by precept but more tellingly by example," writes Bishop Tutu.[488] Other similar stories available throughout the literature on reconciliation provide hopeful illustrations of the power of reconciliation to right old wrongs, overcome past injustice, forge new futures, and reunite individuals, groups, and nations.

The third goal for individual transformation is that participants will empathize with others as prerequisite to reconciliation practices. From psychology's perspective on forgiveness, Enright and Fitzgibbons suggest that in the "work phase" of forgiveness, clients may find that "it is often easier to understand an offender than it is to feel empathy or compassion for him or her."[489] However, the authors continue, "Following cognitive decisions to forgive and insight, emotional transformations toward the offender may emerge. . . . The key is that the client is seeing the offender in new ways and may become ready to respond in new ways."[490] In addition, the Enright and Fitzgibbons allow for compassion in which the offended "suffers along with the injurer" because they see the injurer as a "vulnerable human being, despite her unjust act or her subsequent response to that act."[491]

Augsburger notes that "reconciliation between self and other requires meeting—the meeting of worlds of experience and perception."[492] One of the perceptions persons can have of those who have offended them is to "recognize and empathize" with them. Recognition allows a person to see similarities and differences between themselves and their offenders. However, empathy "invites us to engage and be engaged by what we do not perceive within ourselves because of its absence or our lack of insight."[493] Moreover,

Augsburger argues that "Embracing the enemy is not a desirable option, it is the optimum goal of reconciliation."[494] One final insight into empathy and reconciliation is offered. Augsburger avers that respect for the other is comprised of two components: empathy and exploration of the truth. The two disputants recognize that in their ability to empathize with one another, they have opened up the new possibility of dealing with issues that before could not have been considered.[495] Helping participants at Chatham Baptist Church empathize with those who are other than they are—particularly in the area of racial reconciliation—will enable new perspectives on this community's centuries-long biases.

A fourth transformative goal is that participants will be able to understand the main themes of reconciliation across disciplines. The themes of reconciliation in psychology, sociology, and peace building studies have already been explored and space does not permit revisiting those distinctions. However, the salient points are first that theology grounds a Christian perspective on reconciliation and that followers of Christ extend the reconciliation they have experienced between God and in community with others to the wider community and world. Secondly, the praxis of reconciliation can be informed by other disciplines such as psychology, sociology, and peace building studies as the context of each situation allows. Finally, reconciliation is a journey of personal and communal transformation which demands that any church that seeks to serve as a reconciling community must transcend the culture in which it is situated to embrace the biblical vision of the purpose of reconciliation, which is God's *shalom* for the world.

Finally, the fifth transforming goal is that participants actually will take part in designing and implementing a community reconciliation project based on what they have learned and experienced during the eight weeks of worship, study, and reflection. Participants will be encouraged to apply their newly-discovered insights to designing a reconciliation project that meets the criteria found in Brent Myers' book, *Walking with the Poor*. Myers identifies nine values that should shape transformational development, and could also be applied to crafting a ministry of reconciliation. Although space does not allow for a full examination of each, their necessity is self-evident. Myers argues, "Relationships that don't work are reflected through the distortion of what are normally positive values." However, when viewed correctly, these values open the possibility of community and individual transformation. These nine values include loyalty, valuing others, compassion, repentance, forgiveness, sharing, equality, justice, and peacemaking.[496]

## Content of the Strategy

Attention turns next to the content of the strategy of the project. The basic component consists of eight weeks of worship experiences in which the gathered congregation of Chatham Baptist Church will pray, read Scripture, sing hymns, hear sermons, and devote their worship hour each week to a different aspect of reconciliation. Congregational Scripture readings will be selected from Old and New Testaments, and across the genres of biblical material including Law, Prophets, Writings, Gospels, History, Epistles, and Apocalyptic books. Hymns and musical selections will contribute to the overall theme of reconciliation. Sermons based on selected Scripture texts taken from the synoptic Gospels and complemented by real-life accounts of reconciliation will provide content for reflection. As a corollary to the worship component, on Wednesday evenings, participants will reflect on the previous Sunday's topic, explore supplementary material, such as the book, *Reconciling All Things: A Christian Vision for Justice, Peace and Healing* by Emmanuel Katongole and Chris Rice,[497] and have opportunity to pray, discuss, and engage with the material in small groups led by a facilitator.

Resources for the eight-week immersion in reconciliation include Scripture passages for sermons taken from the synoptic Gospels. In keeping with the reimagined ecclesiology of Jesus as hermeneutical center at Chatham Baptist Church, the choice of Jesus' teachings on reconciliation is both instructive and intentional. The eight weeks of topics, although not necessarily final titles, for sermons and their texts are "The Rule of Christ," Matthew 18:15-20; "Fellowship, Repentance, and Restitution in the Story of Zacchaeus," Luke 19:1-10; "Empathy for an Enemy in the Story of the Good Samaritan," Luke 10:25-37; "Repentance, Forgiveness, and Celebration in the Story of the Prodigal Son," Luke 15:11-31; "The Greatest Commandments: Love God, Love Your Neighbor," Matthew 23:34-40; "Baptism and the Lord's Supper as Rituals of Reconciliation,"

Matthew 3:13-17 and Matthew 26:17-30; "The Lord's Prayer and the Necessity of Forgiveness," Matthew 6:5-15; and "You Are Witnesses As the Vocation of the Missional Church," Luke 24:36-49.

In addition, sermons and small group discussions will also use selected literature covering ecclesiology, the missional church, and reconciliation featured in the preparation of this book. Finally, selected audio-visual media will be screened, such as the video presentation, *The Power of Forgiveness*, which features well-known peace and spirituality advocates and real stories of forgiveness in different cultural settings.[498]

An additional component of the eight-week study will be a review of existing models of reconciliation projects in order to aid the participants in designing their own reconciliation project. Some of these existing models will include the Center for Reconciliation at Duke University in Durham, North Carolina; the Center for Justice and Peacebuilding at Eastern Mennonite University in Harrisonburg, Virginia; and local organizations engaged in aspects of community reconciliation such as Third Chance Ministries in Danville, Virginia. In addition, secular institutions such as The Danville Regional Foundation, which promote the well-being of persons and communities within Danville and Pittsylvania County, Virginia, will also be a resource.

## Leadership for the Strategy

Leadership for the strategy will consist of the pastor of Chatham Baptist Church, who will coordinate the project and design its learning components. In the eight weeks of worship services, planning for those services will involve the choir director and choir; persons selected to offer prayer, read Scripture, and present the children's sermon each week; and those who provide support for the services, such as the administrative assistant who prepares the worship programs, the ushers who greet worshippers as they arrive, and the congregation itself. On Wednesday nights, selected members of Chatham Baptist Church will serve as small group facilitators to guide the discussion and group work associated with reflecting on the previous Sunday's topic. Finally, conversation partners from Duke University's Center for Reconciliation, Eastern Mennonite

University's Center for Justice and Peacebuilding, and local representatives from previously mentioned institutions and organizations will be asked to present during the Wednesday evening small group sessions.

## Target Population

The target population of this project is the worshipping congregation of Chatham Baptist Church in Chatham, Virginia. Each Sunday approximately eighty children, teens, and adults gather for worship, and it is this group that will experience the worship component. On Wednesday nights, however, adults will comprise the small groups because youth and children are engaged in ongoing age-specific programs. However, children, youth, and adults will have the opportunity to participate in the community reconciliation project as appropriate. Prior to the entire church congregational experience, a pilot project consisting of selected adults will meet and preview the material. Chapter 7 will offer a complete overview of the pilot project phase.

## Conclusion

In this chapter, three theological implications for a reconciling community have been examined. These include the idea that Chatham Baptist Church will be a witness to reconciliation in and through itself to the world. The second implication is that a ministry of reconciliation can be a bridge from the church's traditional past to its missional future. Third, the church will then understand itself as a community of the reconciled, extending reconciliation to its community and the world.

The preferred future for a ministry of reconciliation at Chatham Baptist Church should involve five criteria: continuity with the best of the church's past; discontinuity with the community's culture of prejudice and estrangement; conversation and confession; humility and trust regarding institutional power; and a shared cross-cultural commitment to work together to transform community institutions including churches, schools, civic clubs, criminal justice agencies, and local businesses. These criteria are concrete actions that can advance and validate the reconciliation process. The final criteria—a shared cross-cultural commitment to transforming community institutions—

moves a ministry of reconciliation away from personal and individual introspection and feelings, into the arena of shared community space in which reconciliation can be conducted and witnessed to by all participants.

In addition to the communal preferred future, goals for individual transformation during the project include affirming a biblical theology of the church as a missional community; embracing the transforming power of reconciliation in relationships; empathizing with others as a prerequisite to reconciliation practices; understanding the main themes of reconciliation across the disciplines surveyed; and participating in designing and implementing a community reconciliation project. These goals are measurable and achievable, and they reflect the transformative nature of the project.

Finally, the content for the eight weeks of worship and reflection is centered upon the teaching of Jesus from the synoptic Gospels. Leadership for the strategy is drawn primarily from the membership of Chatham Baptist Church, with the pastor as project coordinator and content designer. The target population is the congregation gathered for worship, although a pilot project will be implemented with a smaller group prior to the church-wide eight-week event. Chapter 7 will describe the pilot project in greater detail.

# CHAPTER 7

# THE IMPLEMENTATION AND EVALUATION PROCESS

This chapter presents the plan for implementing and evaluating the strategy. A pilot project consisting of worship and small group reflection will become the model for future church-wide sessions while also testing the thesis. Because the strategy involves both an eight-week learning component and a resulting reconciliation action project, two evaluation approaches will be used. First, a pre-test will be completed by participants in the worship and study sessions in order to measure knowledge, attitudes, and experiences. At the end of the eight weeks of study, a post-event survey will provide data for comparing participants' transformation in knowledge, attitudes, and experiences. A separate evaluation will include an instrument to be completed by participants in the community-wide reconciliation project. Finally, at the end of the pilot project, a report will be made to church leadership summarizing the content, findings, and experiences of the pilot project.

## Pilot Project Summary

The pilot project phase will follow the same basic design as the church-wide project, but on a smaller scale. Rather than the target audience of participants being the entire worshipping congregation of Chatham Baptist Church, a select group of twelve to sixteen adults will be invited by the pastor to take part in the pilot project. These twelve to sixteen participants should be representative of the adult members of the congregation in both age and gender. Race might also be a criterion for representation, but as of the writing of this book, all adult members are White.

Leadership for the pilot project will consist of a steering committee, invited by the pastor, and the pastor will act as project coordinator and content editor. The steering committee members will be part of the twelve to sixteen total participants in the pilot project. The purpose of the steering committee is to assist in the logistics of the project such as room preparation, equipment setup and operation, group communication, and facilitation of the breakout groups during the small group reflection time.

The format for the pilot project will be a combination of worship and small group reflection as mentioned in Chapter 6, but with adaptation made in several areas. First, the meeting time for the pilot project group will be on a weeknight, rather than on Sundays and Wednesdays. The reason for a separate meeting time, different from the regular worship hours of the church, is that this is a pilot project, and regular worship and Wednesday night Bible study for adults will continue while the pilot project is in process. The second adaptation is that there will be one meeting time for the pilot project group, which will begin with the worship component, followed by a break, and then time for small group reflection. This enables pilot project participants to complete each session in meetings held one night per week over the eight-week period. Two hours for each meeting will be allotted, which will be equivalent to the time allotted for the church-wide event.

The smaller group will also require that the worship component be changed to a format more appropriate for twelve to sixteen persons, versus the church-wide worship component, which can be expected to include sixty or more adults. The group will probably sit in a circle, rather than in rows, in order to facilitate eye contact and participation. While the reading of Scripture may be the same for the smaller pilot group, the musical selections may come from recordings selected to fit the theme for the evening. The sermon portion of the worship component during the pilot project will be presented by the pastor seated in the circle of participants, rather than standing at a lectern. Other elements of worship may also be adapted with a smaller group of participants in mind.

Although the number of participants, leadership, and format will be adapted for the pilot project, the goal of the eight weeks of worship and reflection remain the same: to conduct a community reconciliation project based on the worship and study experience. However, the project itself may also be scaled appropriately for a smaller group, and might employ a methodology appropriate to an informal setting. One possible methodology that would lend itself well to the pilot project phase is circle processes. Kay Pranis, in her book, *The Little Book of Circle Processes: A New/Old Approach to Peacemaking*, describes the "Circle" and its potential: "Participants sit in a circle of chairs with no tables. Sometimes objects that have meaning to the group are placed in the center as a focal point to remind participants of shared values and common ground. The physical format of the Circle symbolizes shared leadership, equality, connection, and inclusion. It also promotes focus, accountability, and participation from all."[499] According to Pranis, circles draw from the tradition of the "Talking Circle" among indigenous people of North America. The Circles is a proven peacemaking methodology that has been used in rural, suburban, and urban communities, particularly in the area of restorative justice.[500] Employing circle processes in the pilot project guarantees that all participants are respected, that everyone gets a chance to talk without interruption, that everyone is equal, and that both spiritual and emotional aspects of individual experience are welcomed.[501] However, regardless of whether circle processes are used or not, the goal of the pilot project remains the same as the church-wide project: to conduct a community reconciliation project of some type.

## Pilot Project Timeline

The timeline for the pilot project involves identifying and recognizing the logical progression of project preparation, and then allowing adequate time for each step to be completed. The first phase involves the completion of the academic research, which forms the basis for this book and the actual project itself. Academic research includes developing a bibliography of materials that offers a consistent and academically rigorous body of knowledge for the exploration of the thesis. The academic research phase is projected to be completed by the end of February 2013.

Next, appropriate materials for the pilot project have to be gathered and prepared. This involves ordering copies of the book, *Reconciling All Things* by Katongole and Rice; preparing sermon manuscripts based on the previously identified Scripture references; selecting appropriate Scripture readings from across the spectrum of biblical genres and experiences; producing handouts for the small group reflection portion of the project; gathering audio-visual resources such as *The Power of Forgiveness* in DVD format; and preparing the pre- and post-event assessment instruments. Allowing three months to gather and prepare these materials means that all should be ready and available by the end of spring 2013, or about the end of May 2013.

Eight weeks in the summer of 2013 would then be allocated to the pilot project worship and small group reflection meetings. These meetings might begin mid- to late June, and conclude eight weeks later, about the middle or end of August 2013. This timeframe allows a buffer of a few weeks before and after the eight weeks of worship and study.

The pilot project's community reconciliation project would follow after allowing an appropriate amount of time to schedule the actual reconciliation project, identify an issue for discussion using circle processes, invite participants, and schedule space and equipment as needed to conduct the reconciliation event. The event itself could be held in an evening, or on a weekend, depending on the schedule of those participating. For the pilot project specifically, the event should be scaled appropriately to the number of participants, and it should provide a narrowly focused indication of how such an event might actually be planned and implemented. Given the preceding schedule, the community reconciliation project could be scheduled approximately four to six weeks after the end of the eight-week worship and study phase, or approximately in early October 2013. Reflection and evaluation of the community reconciliation project itself should take place at the close of the experience as a type of debriefing and critique of the experience.

## Leadership

As previously noted, leadership for both the pilot project and the church-wide project will come from adult members of Chatham Baptist Church. The pastor will serve as coordinator and content editor for the both phases of the project. The rationale for pastoral leadership is two-fold. First, the pastor has been engaged in researching and writing on the topic of reconciliation during his Doctor of Ministry program. While the pastor is not an expert, the coursework, research, and writing has given him a unique familiarity with the subject matter and resources available on the topic of Christian reconciliation. Second, the congregation has been aware of and supported the pastor in his Doctor of Ministry studies, and the congregation's expectation is that his leadership would be appropriate for this particular project.

As coordinator, the pastor will invite twelve adult participants to serve on a steering committee. The persons invited to serve on the steering committee should be representative of the makeup of the congregation of Chatham Baptist Church in two categories: age and gender. Steering committee participants would include young adults, median adults, and senior adults, with a slightly larger representation of women than men because at present the adults in the congregation are composed of approximately 60 percent women. However, in addition to age and gender, steering committee participant selection also should include length of membership at Chatham Baptist Church, enthusiasm for the church's ministries and the church's future, and regular participation in the life of the congregation. The deacons of Chatham Baptist Church could make up the steering committee, as this group of nine adults is representative of the congregation with the exception that there are only three women currently serving. However, the advantages to asking both current and former deacons to form the steering committee is that as a group they are highly involved with the life of the church, are enthusiastic about the present and future potential of the church, and are supportive of the pastor's leadership and his Doctor of Ministry studies. Furthermore, deacons are selected by the congregation, giving their leadership congregational legitimacy. Since only nine deacons serve at a time, past deacons could be chosen to help balance the age and gender makeup, to assure that it is representative of the congregation. The responsibilities of the steering committee include communicating pertinent information to the congregation; designing the worship and small group reflection aspects of the project; attending to logistical issues such as room preparation, equipment setup, and operation; and insuring that the appropriate materials for each session are prepared and available.

Other leaders for the church-wide project also would include conversation partners from outside institutions such as Duke University's Center for Reconciliation, Eastern Mennonite University's Center for Justice and Peacebuilding, and from local organizations such as Third Chance Ministries, located in Danville, Virginia. These presenters would be invited to share the mission and scope of their respective programs, and how local churches might utilize the resources made available through their institutions. The intent would be to demonstrate that other institutions are addressing the issue of reconciliation, and to become familiar with resources available from these three groups, all located within two to three hours' drive from Chatham, Virginia.

## Resources

Resources necessary for both the pilot project and the church-wide event include space, media, leaders' materials, participants' materials, and creative materials for small group reflection. In terms of space, the church-wide project would utilize the church's sanctuary for the Sunday morning worship component. As the sanctuary is the location for Sunday worship services, this space will be available, and people have already been assigned responsibility for preparing it properly for worship. The Wednesday night small group component would use the church's fellowship hall, with adults remaining around the tables after the regular Wednesday night fellowship meal which takes place each week from September through May. The meal begins at 5:30, with children and teens leaving for their programs at 6:15 PM. Adults then remain in the fellowship hall for adult Bible study and prayer, and that is when the project's small group component would meet.

Media and equipment involved for Sundays includes the usual complement of piano, organ, and audio sound system. The church does not use projection during its traditional worship services on Sunday mornings. However, for the Wednesday night small group experience, a computer and projection screen will be set up for showing video clips from *The Power of Forgiveness* and other selected DVDs. The church will need to secure the appropriate video license to show these DVDs.

Leader materials for both Sunday morning and Wednesday night should be prepared a week in advance, and worship leaders and small group facilitators should be trained in their use, as appropriate for each setting. Sunday worship leader materials include the order of worship, Scripture readings and prayers, and musical selections for choir and guest musicians. Leader materials for Wednesday night small groups include small group facilitation guides with questions for discussion and small group activities to aid in reflection on the topic of the previous Sunday's sermon. Copies of the book, *Reconciling All Things*, by Katongole and Rice, should be available at least one week prior to the first small group session, and small group facilitators should be given their copies two weeks in advance.

Participant materials include copies of *Reconciling All Things*, and handouts prepared to aid in note-taking and small group discussions. In addition, creative materials such as poster board, flip charts, markers, masking tape, and other materials needed for small group interaction should be purchased in the quantities needed for the entire project prior to the beginning of both the pilot project and the church-wide event. A common resource area should be designated where these creative supplies, along with books, DVDs, handouts, and other resources could be organized by session and stored for easy access. The church administrative assistant could be responsible for gathering, organizing, and distributing these materials to appropriate leaders each week.

## Assessment and Evaluation

In order to assess both the pilot project and the church-wide event, identical pre-event and post-event instruments will be used to evaluate the transformation in the knowledge, attitudes, and experiences of participants. Specifically, the instrument should assess individual change in the five goals for individual transformation described in Chapter 6. These goals include affirming a biblical theology of church as a missional community, embracing the transforming power of reconciliation in relationships, empathizing with others as prerequisite to reconciliation practices, understanding the main themes of reconciliation across disciplines, and participating in designing and implementing a community reconciliation project. The anticipated outcome is that participants will be transformed in their knowledge, attitudes, and experiences concerning reconciliation, particularly in their role as members of Chatham Baptist Church.

The design of the assessment instrument will measure the individual participant's agreement or disagreement with specific statements. Five gradations of response using numbered ranges from one to five include: 1-strongly disagree, 2-disagree, 3-neither agree nor disagree, 4-agree, 5-strongly agree. By giving participants a range of responses, even slight change can be detected when the pre-event assessment is compared to the post-event assessment. The pre-event assessment will be administered on the first Sunday of the eight-week series, prior to the start of the worship service. The post-event assessment will be administered on the last Sunday, at the close of the worship service but before the congregation is sent out. The pastor will give instruction for taking both the pre-event and post-event assessments, and ushers will distribute the surveys, and then collect them upon completion. The pastor will catalog the results. Identifying criteria that will assist in evaluating which groupings of members were more or less transformed in their knowledge, attitude, and experiences include length of time as a member of Chatham Baptist Church; gender; and age in ranges corresponding to the "Age Distribution of Chatham Baptist, U. S. Worshippers, and U. S. Population" in Table 1 contained in Chapter 2. The age ranges are fifteen to twenty-four, twenty-five to forty-four, forty-five to sixty-four, and sixty-five and older. With these three identifying criteria, the surveys can be cross-referenced in several ways to assess if a group or groups were more or less changed than other groups. In other words, individual transformation can be charted by age group, length of membership group, gender group, and the congregation as a whole.

A separate evaluation instrument will be administered at the close of the community reconciliation project. This assessment will focus on how participants themselves judge the design, effectiveness, and outcomes of the community reconciliation project. Because the community reconciliation project will be evaluated by both Chatham

Baptist Church members who participated in the eight-week worship and small group phase, and those in the community who did not, the assessment will focus on the outcome of the participants and their perception of the project, not on their personal transformation in knowledge, attitude, and experiences with reconciliation. After the written evaluation of the community reconciliation project, the pastor as director of the community reconciliation project will give an opportunity for participants to share their perception of the experience with the wider group.

## Report on Results of the Learning Component and Reconciliation Project

Within two weeks of the conclusion of both the worship and small group phase, and the community reconciliation project, the project steering committee will prepare a report for church leadership. Church leaders invited to the report presentation and discussion include the church's currently-serving deacons; director of Sunday School; chairs of the Music, Finance, Personnel, Children's and Youth, Food Services, and Building and Grounds committees; Women's Missionary Union president; and church trustees. The report will include a brief description of the design and content of the project, the design and content of the community reconciliation project, and the results of the assessment instruments employed. A report to the congregation gathered on Sunday morning will be presented on the Sunday after the report to church leadership. The report will be presented as an information-only report, but the congregation may be told that in light of the report and the overall experience, specific church committees may bring recommendations for church action at future church business meetings. Whatever the outcome of the report to leaders and the full congregation, the members of Chatham Baptist Church should be commended for undertaking the risk of exploring how the church might become a missional community of reconciliation. Opportunities for continued discussion would then be provided during the next two Wednesday night meetings, as a way of reflecting on the entire experience and how the church has been transformed by it.

## Conclusion

In conclusion, the implementation and evaluation process will test the thesis that Chatham Baptist Church can reimagine itself as a missional community of reconciliation. By carefully detailing the pilot project, leadership, content, church-wide project design, and providing opportunities for evaluation, the congregation of Chatham Baptist Church will have a systematic mechanism for exploring a new possibility for its future identity and ministry. Whatever the outcome, the experience can be compared to the nation of Israel traveling through the wilderness to the Promised Land. While there may be detours, distractions, and failures along the way, the desire of Chatham Baptist Church to reimagine itself in accord with the will of God for its future is in itself something to celebrate.

# SUMMARY AND CONCLUSION

The thesis of this book is that an old congregation founded in 1857, called Chatham Baptist Church, can reimagine itself as a missional community of reconciliation by learning about reconciliation during worship and small group experiences, and then by demonstrating the practice of reconciliation through a church-initiated community reconciliation project. Given the context of the surrounding community, its history of slavery from the early seventeenth century, the oppression of former slaves during Reconstruction, and the invidious discrimination of Jim Crow laws in the twentieth century, there is much that needs reconciling in Chatham, Danville, and Pittsylvania County, Virginia. Moreover, the church itself faces challenges to its existence such as an aging membership, declining community population, and the uncertainty of its own mission. However, the church does have a rich history of creating four significant community institutions: Hargrave Military Academy, Samuel Harris Baptist Church, The Boys and Girls Club of Chatham, and The Community Center at Chatham. The focus of this book is that the church can build upon its demonstrated concern for its community, evidenced in the founding of the four institutions, and leverage that history toward creating a new future for itself and its community—a future of reconciled relationships across racial and cultural barriers.

In order to reimagine itself as a missional community of reconciliation, this book has suggested that the church attend to three areas in its transformation. The first area was its own historic ecclesiology. Using the five Baptist freedoms identified by Baptist historian Walter Shurden, and informed by the witness of Anabaptist history and theology, the church is able to first reimagine its ecclesiology. The hyper-individualism of soul freedom is translated into a more communal focus of Chatham Baptist Church as a faith community gathered around Jesus and sent by him into the world. Secondly, instead of the isolation of church freedom's autonomy, Chatham Baptist Church could re-vision its autonomy into the freedom to cooperate and collaborate with local agencies, groups, and individuals to craft its own ministry of reconciliation.

Third, the prized privilege of Bible freedom among Southern Baptists could be expanded and transformed to encourage the church to read Scripture as a community with Jesus Christ as the hermeneutical center. Fourth, rather than religious freedom being co-opted by twenty-first century party politics, the church could exercise its privilege of religious freedom to witness to the civil and secular institutional authorities within its ministry area. Finally, rather than the church's mission being understood as support for the denomination's missions programs, the church could reinvent its mission as a community of the reconciled witnessing to its community and the world of God's reconciling love.

The second area the church must attend to is grounding its ministry of reconciliation theologically, while informing its praxis of reconciliation with the insights of the disciplines of forgiveness studies in psychology, race and ethnicity studies in sociology, and peace building studies. By studying and discussing the biblical material from both Old and New Testaments regarding reconciliation, the church can expand its theological imagination from its Southern Baptist's roots to embrace a wider concern about the *missio Dei*—God reconciling all of creation. With a solid theological foundation, the church can then understand from other disciplines the dynamics, parameters, and perspectives on reconciliation that each offers.

The third area that the church must attend to is that of transforming the church from a congregation with a mission to a community as mission. The terminology of the missional church conversation is helpful, and the church could understand that it exists not for itself, but for the life of the world. By living out of the mystery of its calling, the memory of its shared past, and allowing those experiences to shape its mission to the world, the church can then become a missional community of reconciliation as its signature ministry to the world.

These three areas are areas of transformation for the church and individuals within the church. As members of the church are transformed by the eight-week worship and study phase, space is created for the church to be transformed in its ecclesiological philosophy, theological praxis, and missional purpose. Moreover, the church can utilize this transformation as a bridge from its tradition Southern Baptist past into a twenty-first century missional future.

Once the church has completed both the pilot project phase and the church-wide event culminating in a community reconciliation project, it will be able to evaluate its calling to the mission of reconciliation. As the church sees its past with new eyes, and envisions its future as a reimagined extension of its history, members will come to appreciate the continuity of the church's life and mission, albeit with new forms and expressions. The implications for the future of the church are that it will have a new intentional missional focus and a new identity in the community, and it will build bridges to individuals, groups, and institutions within the community and world who share a similar vision of reconciled relationships and God's *shalom*.

However, this journey toward becoming a missional community of reconciliation is not important just for one congregation in a small rural community in Virginia. The transformation Chatham Baptist Church anticipates has implications for the wider Christian community. David Fitch, in his book, *The End of Evangelicalism? Discerning a New Faithfulness for Mission*, arrives at a similar conclusion as this book, although by a much different route. Fitch articulates the purpose of his book by stating, "The task that lies ahead in this brief book is to analyze what happened here [in evangelicalism's loss of its core meaning] and then to reorient evangelical belief and practice for the political task of shaping communities into God's mission in the world."[502] Fitch critiques evangelicalism and its expression as an "empty politic." The challenge, Fitch argues, is that evangelicalism must reimagine itself with "a politic of fullness," which means "the politic that is founded in the triune God's work in the world—the politic of reconciliation and peace offered in and through the Incarnate Son."[503]

In a chapter titled "Recovering the Core of Our Politics for Mission: Towards an Evangelical Missional Political Theology," Fitch articulates a vision of evangelicalism as it reimagines its three basic tenets: the inerrant Bible, the decision for Christ, and the Christian nation.[504] Using the cultural theory of Slavoj Zizek, Fitch develops his thesis that evangelicalism is "an empty politic," but that there is a way of life together in Christian community that is a "politic of fullness."[505] Although space does not permit a full review of Fitch's involved and detailed argument, his point about evangelicalism parallels the experience of Chatham Baptist Church: old forms of familiar faith are not sufficient for the challenges of twenty-first century contexts. Fitch sums up his argument by sketching its parameters:

> As opposed to the way the public has caricatured us [evangelicals], I show how these beliefs ["the authority of Scripture, a conversionist salvation, and an activist evangelistic stance of the church in the world"[506]] can and should shape our lives communally for incarnational presence, authentic witness, hospitable engagement, and the daily inhabitation of God's mission (*missio Dei*) in the world. This is what an evangelical political theology should do: orient our lives into God's mission.[507]

Fitch understands the essence of Christian community and the mission of God as reconciliation because "the Christian life in community is driven by reconciliation, not conflict."[508] Further, Fitch continues, "This reconciliation has already been inaugurated by God in the incarnate work of the Son sent into the world. He is our peace (Romans 5:1-10). As opposed to Zizek's conflictual politic, the Christian politic is constituted here in the reconciliation founded in Christ."[509] However, Fitch does not leave the idea of an evangelical politic as a theoretical proposition. Rather, the stance that Fitch suggests the church adopt is "a politic of humble presence, faithfulness, and compassion in the world that comes from this ontological participation in Christ."[510] He further adds that "as evangelicals, we must undo the ways our beliefs and practices have become separated from the ongoing work of God in Christ for the world."[511] The evangelical Church does this by reimaging its core beliefs and by "re-grounding these three commitments [Bible, decision, and nation] politically in the triune work of God through Christ by the Spirit" which will then "shape evangelicals participation in his [God's] mission in the world."[512]

Fitch, in other words, is calling for a rethinking and re-grounding of core theological beliefs in order to better situate evangelicalism in the mission of God. This is exactly the same argument this book makes in calling for the ecclesiology of Chatham Baptist Church to be reimagined in order to create a more hospitable environment for the church to become a missional community of reconciliation. However, Fitch does not stop there, but continues to press for evangelicalism's transformation into a missional movement. He writes,

> "Along the way, subtly, evangelicalism as an ideology 'de-missionalized' the church, setting its drives, desires, and political existence at odds with the mission of God. We took on an exclusivist, duplicitous and dispassionate posture in the world. Re-grounding these three doctrinal commitments as described above should reverse these effects."[513]

Fitch also concurs that the church gathers for worship "to be shaped together into his body for the world. We practice the Eucharist, thereby becoming a reconciled people carrying the forgiveness and new life of God's salvific work 'in Christ' into the world."[514] Finally, Fitch sums up the role of the Church as a reconciling community: "The communal nature of this reality does not separate us from the world. Rather, by becoming the very righteousness of God (2 Cor. 5:21), we can humbly, vulnerably incarnate justice and reconciliation in the world."[515] That is the argument of this book.

However, this book is more than a theoretical argument. The story contained here has implications for Chatham Baptist Church, and by extension, other churches reimagining themselves as missional communities of reconciliation. The stories of estrangement are contained not only in the Bible, but in the lived experiences of churches today. The dream that these stories can have a different ending is promising for both churches and evangelicalism itself.

Should the vision of reconciliation become a reality and create the "beloved community"[516] of which Dr. King spoke, then the congregation of Chatham Baptist Church, and other churches which embrace that vision, will have a new story to tell to the generations to come: "All of this is from God, who reconciled us to himself through Christ and gave us the ministry of reconciliation" (2 Corinthians 5:18). That would be a story worth passing on to the children of this church and its community.

# BIBLIOGRAPHY

Aaron, Larry G. *Pittsylvania County Virginia: A Brief History*. Charleston, SC: The History Press, 2009.

Alley, Reuben Edward. *A History of Baptists in Virginia*. Richmond, VA: Virginia Baptist General Board, 1973.

Anderson, Ray S. *The Shape of Practical Theology: Empowering Ministry with Theological Praxis*. Downers Grove, IL: InterVarsity Press, 2001.

Augsburger, David W. *Helping People Forgive*. Louisville, KY: Westminster John Knox Press, 1996.

_____. *Conflict Mediation Across Cultures: Pathways and Patterns*. Louisville, KY: Westminster John Knox Press, 1992.

_____. *Dissident Discipleship: A Spirituality of Self-Surrender, Love of God, and Love of Neighbor*. Grand Rapids, MI: Brazos Press, 2006.

_____. *The New Freedom of Forgiveness*, 3rd ed. Chicago: Moody Publishers, 2000.

Aylor, Ella Vaden. *Centennial of the Chatham Baptist Church: 1857-1957*. Chatham, VA: Star-Tribune, 1957.

Battle, Michael. *Reconciliation: The Ubuntu Theology of Desmond Tutu*. Rev. ed. Cleveland: Pilgrim Press, 2009.

Baum, Gregory and Harold Wells, eds. *The Reconciliation of Peoples: Challenge to the Churches*. Eugene, OR: Wipf & Stock, 2009.

Bebbington, David W. *Baptists through the Centuries: A History of a Global People*. Waco, TX: Baylor University Press, 2012.

Bender, Harold S. *The Anabaptist Vision*. Scottdale, PA: Herald Press, 1994.

Birch, Bruce C., Walter Brueggemann, Terence E. Fretheim, and

David L. Petersen. *A Theological Introduction to the Old Testament.* 2nd ed. Nashville: Abingdon Press, 2005.

Blair, William A. *Cities of the Dead: Contesting the Memory of the Civil War in the South, 1865-1914.* Chapel Hill, NC: The University of North Carolina Press, 2004. Kindle Electronic Edition.

Bloom, Harold. *The American Religion.* 2nd ed. New York: Chu Hartley Publishers, 2006.

Bonhoeffer, Dietrich. *Dietrich Bonhoeffer Works, Volume I, Sanctorum Communio: A Theological Study of the Sociology of the Church.* Translated by Reinhard Krauss and Nancy Lukens. Minneapolis: Fortress Press, 1998.

Bonilla-Silva, Eduardo. *Racism Without Racists: Color-Blind Racism & Racial Inequality in Contemporary America.* 3rd ed. New York: Rowman & Littlefield Publishers, Inc., 2010.

Bosch, David J. *Transforming Mission: Paradigm Shifts in Theology of Mission.* Maryknoll, NY: Orbis Books, 2007.

Braver, Barbara, ed. *I Have Called You Friends: Reflections on Reconciliation: In Honor of Frank T. Griswold.* Cambridge, MA: Cowley Publications, 2006.

Brueggemann, Walter. *Deep Memory, Exuberant Hope: Contested Truth in a Post-Christian World.* Minneapolis: Fortress Press, 2000.

_____. *Peace.* St. Louis, MO: Chalice Press, 2001.

Buttrick, George Arthur, ed. *The Interpreter's Dictionary of the Bible: An Illustrated Encyclopedia*, Volume 4. Nashville: Abingdon Press, 1962.

Chaves, Mark. *Congregations in America.* Cambridge, MA: Harvard University Press, 2004.

Chatham Baptist Church. *1969 Handbook.* Chatham, VA: Chatham

Baptist Church, 1969.

_____. *Constitution and By-laws*. Chatham, VA: Chatham Baptist Church, 2006.

_____. *Policies and Procedures Manual*. Chatham, VA: Chatham Baptist Church, 2006.

Cooperrider, David L. and Diana Whitney. *Appreciative Inquiry: A Positive Revolution in Change*. San Francisco: Berrett-Koehler Publishers, Inc., 2005.

Coward, Harold and Gordon S. Smith, eds. *Religion and Peacebuilding*. Albany, NY: State University of New York Press, 2004.

Cox, Brian. *Faith-Based Reconciliation: A Moral Vision That Transforms People and Societies*. Lexington, KY: Xlibris Corporation, 2007.

Daly, Erin and Jeremy Sarkin. *Reconciliation in Divided Societies: Finding Common Ground*. Philadelphia: University of Pennsylvania Press, 2007.

de Gruchy, John W. *Reconciliation: Restoring Justice*. Minneapolis: Fortress Press, 2002.

De La Torre, Miguel. *Liberating Jonah: Forming an Ethics of Reconciliation*. Maryknoll, NY: Orbis Books, 2007.

DeYmaz, Mark. *Building a Healthy Multi-Ethnic Church: Mandate, Commitments, and Practices of a Diverse Congregation*. San Francisco: Jossey-Bass, 2007.

Emerson, Michael O. and Christian Smith. *Divided by Faith: Evangelical Religion and the Problem of Race in America*. New York: Oxford University Press, 2000. Kindle Electronic Edition.

Emerson, Michael O. and Rodney M. Woo. *People of the Dream: Multiracial Congregations in the United States*. Princeton University Press, 2006.

Enright, Robert D. and Richard P. Fitzgibbons. *Helping Clients Forgive: An Empirical Guide for Resolving Anger and Restoring Hope.* Washington, D. C.: American Psychological Association, 2000.

Estep, William R. *The Anabaptist Story: An Introduction to Sixteenth-Century Anabaptism.* 3rd ed. Grand Rapids, MI: William B. Eerdmans Publishing Company, 1996.

_____. *Whole Gospel, Whole World: The Foreign Mission Board of the Southern Baptist Convention 1845-1995.* Nashville: Broadman and Holman Publishers, 1994.

Fitch, David E. *The End of Evangelicalism? Discerning a New Faithfulness for Mission: Towards an Evangelical Political Theology.* Eugene, OR: Cascade Books, 2011. Kindle Electronic Edition.

Furr, Gary A. and Curtis W. Freeman, eds. *Ties That Bind: Life Together in the Baptist Vision.* Macon, GA: Smyth and Helwys Publishing, Inc., 1994.

Galindo, Israel. *The Hidden Lives of Congregations: Discerning Church Dynamics.* Herndon, VA: The Alban Institute, 2004.

Garrett, James Leo. *Baptist Theology: A Four-Century Study.* Macon, GA: Mercer University Press, 2009.

Gourley, Bruce T. *Diverging Loyalties: Baptists in Middle Georgia during the Civil War.* Macon, GA: Mercer University Press, 2011.

Grimsrud, Ted. *Embodying the Way of Jesus: Anabaptist Convictions for the Twenty-first Century.* Eugene, OR: Wipf and Stock Publishers, 2007.

Guder, Darrell L., ed. *Missional Church: A Vision for the Sending of the Church in North America.* Grand Rapids, MI: Wm. B. Eerdmans Publishing Co., 1998.

Hays, Richard B. *The Moral Vision of the New Testament: Community, Cross, New Creation: A Contemporary Introduction to New Testament Ethics.*

New York: HarperCollins Publishers, 1996.

Heywood, Linda M. and John K. Thornton. *Central Africans, Atlantic Creoles, and the Foundation of the Americas, 1585-1660*. New York: Cambridge University Press, 2007.

Hobbs, Herschel H. *The Baptist Faith and Message*. Rev. ed. Nashville: Convention Press, 2004.

Humphreys, Fisher. *The Way We Were: How Southern Baptist Theology Has Changed and What It Means To Us All*. Macon, GA: Smyth & Helwys Publishing, Inc., 2002.

Jobs for the Future. *Report to the Danville Regional Foundation: Assessment of Workforce Development and Related Educational Challenges and Opportunities*. Boston: Jobs for the Future, 2007.

Jones, Gregory L. *Embodying Forgiveness: A Theological Analysis*. Grand Rapids, MI: Wm. B. Eerdmans Publishing Company, 1995.

Kalayjian, Ani, and Raymond F. Paloutzian. *Forgiveness and Reconciliation: Psychological Pathways to Conflict Transformation and Peace Building*. New York: Springer Science+Business Media, LLC, 2010.

Karkkainen, Veli-Matti. *Introduction to Ecclesiology: Ecumenical, Historical and Global Perspectives*. Downers Grove, IL: InterVarsity Press, 2002.

Kantongole, Emmanuel and Chris Rice. *Reconciling All Things: A Christian Vision for Justice, Peace and Healing*. Downers Grove, IL; InterVarsity Press, 2008. Kindle Electronic Edition.

Kaufman, Will. *The Civil War in American Culture*. Edinburgh: Edinburgh University Press, 2006.

King, Martin Luther, Jr. *I Have a Dream: Writings and Speeches That Changed the World*. Edited by James Melvin Washington. New York: Harper One, 1992.

Klassen, William. *The Forgiving Community*. Philadelphia: The Westminster Press, 1966.

Kraus, C. Norman, ed. *The Community of the Spirit: How the Church Is in the World*. Rev. ed. Eugene, OR: Wipf & Stock, 2007.

_____. *Evangelicalism and Anabaptism*. Eugene, OR: Wipf and Stock Publishers, 1979.

Kreider, Alan, Eleanor Kreider, and Paulus Widjaja. *A Culture of Peace: God's Vision for the Church*. Intercourse, PA: Good Books, 2005.

Lassiter, Matthew D., and Andrew B. Lewis, eds. *The Moderates' Dilemma: Massive Resistance to School Desegregation in Virginia*. Charlottesville, VA: University Press of Virginia, 1998.

Lederach, John Paul. *Building Peace: Sustainable Reconciliation in Divided Societies*. Washington, D. C.: United States Institute of Peace Press, 1997.

_____. *The Moral Imagination: The Art and Soul of Building Peace*. New York: Oxford University Press, Inc., 2005.

Leek, Chas. F. *The History of the Pittsylvania Baptist Association: 1788-1963*. Danville, VA: The Pittysylvania Baptist Association, 1963.

Leonard, Bill J. *Baptist Ways: A History*. Valley Forge, PA: Judson Press, 2003.

Livingston, James C. *Anatomy of the Sacred: An Introduction to Religion*. 6th ed. Upper Saddle River, NJ: Pearson Prentice Hall, 2009.

Marsh, Charles. *The Beloved Community: How Faith Shapes Social Justice, from the Civil Rights Movement to Today*. New York: Basic Books, 2005.

Massey, Douglas S. *Categorically Unequal: The American Stratification System*. New York: Russell Sage Foundation, 2007.

McClendon, James Wm. *Doctrine: Systematic Theology, Volume II.* Nashville: Abingdon Press, 1994.

⎯⎯⎯⎯⎯⎯⎯⎯. *Ethics: Systematic Theology, Volume I.* Rev. ed. Nashville: Abingdon Press, 2002.

⎯⎯⎯⎯⎯⎯⎯⎯. "What Is Southern Baptist Ecumenism?" *Southwestern Journal of Theology* 10 (Spring 1968): 73.

Mullins, E. Y. *The Axioms of Religion.* Macon, GA: Mercer University Press, 2010.

Myers, Bryant L. *Walking with the Poor: Principles and Practices of Transformational Development.* Maryknoll, NY: Orbis Books, 1999.

Noll, Mark A. *American Evangelical Christianity: An Introduction.* Malden, MA: Blackwell Publishers Inc., 2001.

⎯⎯⎯⎯⎯⎯⎯⎯. *The Civil War as a Theological Crisis.* Chapel Hill, NC: The University of North Carolina Press, 2006. Kindle Electronic Edition.

⎯⎯⎯⎯⎯⎯⎯⎯. *God and Race in American Politics: A Short History.* Princeton University Press, 2008.

Okholm, Dennis, ed. *The Gospel in Black and White: Theological Resources for Racial Reconciliation.* Downers Grove, IL: InterVarsity Press, 1997.

Oldenburg, Ray. *The Great Good Place: Cafes, Coffee Shops, Bookstores, Bars, Hair Salons, and Other Hangouts at the Heart of a Community.* New York: Marlowe & Company, 1999.

Parillo, Vincent N. *Understanding Race and Ethnic Relations.* 4th ed. Boston: Allyn and Bacon, 2012.

Pearce, Edward. *Pitt the Elder: Man of War.* London: The Bodley Head Random House, 2010. Kindle Electronic Edition.

Pittsylvania Baptist Association. *2010 Annual of the Pittsylvania Baptist Association.* Danville, VA: Pittsylvania Baptist Association, 2010.

Pinder, Sherrow O. *Whiteness and Racialized Ethnic Groups in the United States: The Politics of Remembering.* Lanham, MD: Lexington Books, 2012.

Pranis, Kay. *The Little Book of Circle Processes: A New/Old Approach to Peacemaking.* Intercourse, PA: Good Books, 2005.

Putnam, Robert D. and David E. Campbell. *American Grace: How Religion Divides and Unites Us.* New York: Simon & Schuster, 2010. Kindle Electronic Edition.

Rah, Soong-Chan. *The Next Evangelicalism: Freeing the Church from Western Cultural Captivity.* Downers Grove, IL: InterVarsity Press, 2009.

Roth, John D., ed. *Engaging Anabaptism: Conversations with a Radical Tradition.* Scottdale, PA: Herald Press, 2001.

Roxburgh, Alan J. *Missional Map-Making: Skills for Leading in Times of Transition.* San Francisco: Jossey-Bass, 2010.

Roxburgh, Alan J. and M. Scott Boren. *Introducing the Missional Church: What It Is, Why It Matters, How To Become One.* Grand Rapids, MI: Baker Books, 2009.

Sawatsky, Jarem. *Justpeace Ethics: A Guide to Restorative Justice and Peacebuilding.* Eugene, OR: Cascade Books, 2008.

Schaller, Lyle E. *Small Congregations, Big Potential: Ministry in the Small Membership Church.* Nashville: Abingdon Press, 2003.

Schreiter, Robert J. *Reconciliation: Mission & Ministry in a Changing Social Order.* Maryknoll, NY: Orbis Books, 1992.

Sherif, Muzafer, O. J. Harvey, B. Jack White, William R. Hood, and Carolyn W. Shief. *The Robbers Cave Experiment: Intergroup Conflict and Cooperation.* Middleton, CT: Wesleyan University Press, 1988.

Shurden, Walter B. *The Baptist Identity: Four Fragile Freedoms*. Macon, GA: Smyth and Helwys Publishing, Inc., 1993.

Siegel, Frederick F. *The Roots of Southern Distinctiveness: Tobacco and Society in Danville, Virginia, 1780-1865*. Chapel Hill, NC: The University of North Carolina Press, 1987.

Smith, Robert Sidney. *Mill on the Dan: A History of Dan River Mills, 1882-1950*. Durham, NC: Duke University Press, 1960.

Stamp, Kenneth M. *The Peculiar Institution: Slavery in the Ante-Bellum South*. 1956. Reprint, New York: Vintage Books, 1989.

Stassen, Glenn H., ed. *Just Peacemaking: The New Paradigm for the Ethics of Peace and War*. Cleveland, OH: The Pilgrim Press, 2008.

_____. *A Thicker Jesus: Incarnational Discipleship in a Secular Age*. Louisville, KY: Westminster John Knox Press, 2012. Kindle Edition.

Stassen, Glen H., and David P. Gushee. *Kingdom Ethics: Following Jesus in Contemporary Context*. Downers Grove, IL: InterVarsity Press, 2003.

Swanson, Michael. *Danville, Virginia and the Coming of the Modern South*. Lexington, KY: CreateSpace, 2010.

Tredway, Page. *Chatham Baptist Church: A Child's Recollection*. Danville, VA: J. T. Townes Ptg. Co., 1967.

Tutu, Desmond Mpilo. *No Future without Forgiveness*. New York: Doubleday, 1999. Kindle Electronic Edition.

Van Gelder, Craig. *The Ministry of the Missional Church: A Community Led by the Spirit*. Grand Rapids, MI: Baker Books, 2007.

Walker, Margaret Urban. *Moral Repair: Reconstructing Moral Relations after Wrongdoing*. New York: Cambridge University Press, 2006.

Wallenstein, Peter. *Cradle of America: Four Centuries of Virginia History*. Lawrence, KS: The University Press of Kansas, 2007.

Warnock, Charles. "Appreciative Inquiry Report and Reflection." Seminar paper, Fuller Theological Seminary, 2006.

_____. "Creating the Future: Leadership and Missional Imagination." Seminar paper, Fuller Theological Seminary, 2006.

_____. "Learn to Partner." Leadership (Spring 2007): 108-11.

Williams, Michael E., Sr. and Walter B. Shurden, eds. *Turning Points in Baptist History: A Festschrift in Honor of Harry Leon McBeth*. Macon, GA: Mercer University Press, 2008.

Wiesel, Elie. *Night*. Translated by Marion Wiesel. New York: Hill and Wang, 2006.

Willimon, William H. *Worship as Pastoral Care*. Nashville: Abingdon Press, 1979.

Woolever, Cynthia and Deborah Bruce. *A Field Guide to U.S. Congregations: Who's Going Where and Why*. Louisville, KY: Westminster John Knox Press, 2002.

Worthington, Everett L., Jr. *Dimensions of Forgiveness: Psychological Research and Theological Perspectives*. Radnor, PA: Templeton Foundation Press, 1998.

Wright, N. T. *The New Testament and the People of God*. Minneapolis: Fortress Press, 1992.

Yoder, John Howard. *Body Politics: Five Practices of the Christian Community Before the Watching World*. Scottdale, PA: Herald Press, 2001.

_____. *He Came Preaching Peace*. Scottdale, PA: Herald Press, 2004.

_____. *The Priestly Kingdom: Social Ethics as Gospel*. University of Notre Dame, 1984.

Yoder, Perry B. Shalom: *The Bible's Word for Salvation, Justice, and Peace*. Nappanee, IN: Evangel Publishing House, 1987.

Yoder, Perry B. and Willard M. Swartley, eds. *The Meaning of Peace: Biblical Studies*. Elkhart, IN: Institute of Mennonite Studies, 2001.

## Websites

Allen, Bob. "Southern Baptists elect black president." Associated Baptist Press. http://abpnews.com/ministry/organizations/item/7540-southern-baptists-elect-black-president#.UQRZBkqjeOE (accessed January 26, 2013).

Association of Religion Data Archives. "County Membership Report, 51143." http://www.thearda.com/mapsReports/reports/counties/51143_2000.asp (accessed January 28, 2012).

_____. "County Membership Report, 51590." http://www.thearda.com/mapsReports/reports/counties/51590_2000.asp (accessed January 28, 2012).

_____. "State Membership Report." http://www.thearda.com/mapsReports/reports/ state/51_2000.asp (accessed January 28, 2012)

Baptist Press. "Press Release: September 3 1960." Southern Baptist History Library and Archives. http://media.sbhla.org.s3.amazonaws.com/1093,03-Sep-1960.pdf (accessed February 10, 2012).

_____. "SBC severs ties with BWA as theological concerns remain." http://www.bpnews.net/bpnews.asp?id=18475 (accessed September 27, 2012).

The Boys and Girls Club of the Danville Area. "Locations and Directions." http://www.bgcdanville.org/index.php?option=com_content&view=article&id=109&Itemid=183 (accessed February 13, 2012).

Chatham Cares, Inc. "About Us." The Community Center at Chatham. http://chathamcares.org/about-us/ (accessed January 28, 2012).

_____. "Building Use." The Community Center at Chatham. http://chathamcares. org/building-use/ (accessed February 13, 2012).

Chuck Warnock. "Chatham Arts Community Music School." Chuck Warnock blog, entry dated May 15, 2007. http://chuckwarnockblog.wordpress.com/2007/05/15/ chatham-arts-community-music-school/ (accessed January 28, 2012).

CNN. "Governor McDonnell Apologizes for Omitting Slavery in Confederacy Proclamation." http://articles.cnn.com/2010-04-07/politics/virginia.confederate. history_1_slavery-apology-confederate-history-month?_s=PM:POLITICS (accessed January 28, 2012).

Country Music Hall of Fame and Museum. "Tom T. Hall." http://countrymusichall offame.org/full-list-of-inductees/view/tom-t-hall (accessed September 27, 2012).

Danville Regional Foundation. "2010 Regional Report Card." http://drfonline.org/region/documents/2011/2010-Regional-Report-Card-summary.pdf (accessed January 28, 2012).

_____. "Danville-Pittsylvania County, VA Census Briefing." http://drfonline.org/documents/CensusBriefingReport2010.pdf (accessed January 28, 2012).

_____."Vision and Mission." http://drfonline.org/about/vision.php (accessed January 28, 2012).

Hargrave Military Academy. "Educational Philosophy." http://www.hargrave. edu/admissions/about-hargrave/educational-philosophy/ (accessed February 13, 2012).

Institute for Advanced Learning and Research. "Home." http://ialr.org/ (accessed January 28, 2012).

Kumar, Anita. "Top McDonnell Supporter Condemns Governor for Confederate History Month." Washington Post. http://voices.washingtonpost.com/virginiapolitics/2010/04/top_mcdonnell_supporter_ condem.html (accessed January 28, 2012).

Kumar, Anita and Rosalind S. Helderman. "McDonnell's Confederate History Month Proclamation Irks Civil Rights Leaders." The Washington Post. http://www. washingtonpost.com/wp-dyn/content/article/2010/04/06/AR2010040604416.html (accessed January 28, 2012).

McDonnell, Bob. "Meet Bob." http://bobmcdonnell.com/meet_bob/ (accessed January 30, 2012).

McKissic, Wm. Dwight Sr. "Lessons From the Animal Kingdom." http://dwightmckissic. wordpress.com/2011/03/12/lessons-from-the-animal-kingdom/ (accessed January 26, 2013).

Morin, Rich. "Rising Share of Americans See Conflict Between Rich and Poor." Pew Research. http://www.pewsocialtrends.org/2012/01/11/rising-share-of-americans-see-conflict-between-rich-and-poor/ (accessed January 28, 2012).

Roach, David. "WRIGHT: Keep Legal Name; Add Informal Descriptor 'Great Commission Baptists." Journal of the Southern Baptist Convention. http:// www. Sbclife.net/Articles/2012/03-/Sla1.asp (accessed September 27, 2012).

Southern Baptist Convention. "Comparison of the 1925, 1963 and 2000 Baptist Faith and Message." http://sbc.org/bfm/bfmcomparison.asp (accessed September 27, 2012).

_____. "Resolution on Racial Reconciliation on the 150th Anniversary of the Southern Baptist Convention."

http://www.sbc.net/resolutions/ amresolution.asp?id=899 (accessed on October 26, 2012).

Thriving Rural Communities. "Rev. Chuck Warnock on How a Small Church Has Made a Big Difference." Duke Divinity School. http://divinity.duke.edu/initiatives-centers/thriving-rural-communities/covered-dish/rev-chuck-warnock (accessed January 28, 2012).

Town of Chatham, Virginia. "Visit Chatham." http://chatham-va.gov/visit-chatham (accessed January 27, 2012).

Virginia Center for Digital History. "Martin Luther King, Jr., Speech, Danville, Virginia (WDBJ Television, Roanoke, VA)." University of Virginia. http://www2.vcdh. virginia.edu/civilrightstv/wdbj/-segments/WDBJ04_25.html (accessed January 27, 2012).

The Virginia Tobacco Indemnification and Community Revitalization Commission. "The Institute for Advanced Learning and Research (IALR)." http://www.tic.virginia. gov/ialr.shtml (accessed January 30, 2012).

# ABOUT THE AUTHOR

Charles H. Warnock is pastor of the historic Chatham Baptist Church in Chatham, Virginia. A graduate of Mercer University (BA), Southwestern Baptist Theological Seminary (MDiv), and Fuller Theological Seminary (DMin), Warnock has served in pastoral ministry for over thirty years, with experience leading small churches, large churches, established churches, and founding a new church.

Warnock has written extensively for publication and was contributing editor for small church concerns at Outreach magazine. His articles have appeared in Outreach magazine, Leadership Journal, Outcomes, Neue, and numerous denominational periodicals. His online articles appear on sites like Ethics Daily, Building Church Leaders, Christianity Today, Sermon Central, Huffington Post, Sojourners, and others. In addition to his writing, Chuck has spoken at national conventions and conferences such as the National Outreach Convention and Billy Graham Schools of Evangelism. Since 2006, his blog, ChuckWarnock.com, has attracted over one-million visitors and is often included among leading church ministry blogs. You can find him on Twitter @chuck_warnock, and on Facebook, Google+, Linked-In, and other social media.

Chuck's wife, Debbie, is an artist. They live in an old Victorian house on Main Street in Chatham where neighbors drop by, and their grandchildren come to visit often.

# ENDNOTES

## Introduction

[1] Jeff Sharlet, author of *The Family: The Secret Fundamentalism at the Heart of American Power*, email interview by author, July 19, 2009.

[2] Will Kaufman, *The Civil War in American Culture* (Edinburgh University Press, 2006), 77.

[3] Martin Luther King, Jr., *I Have a Dream: Writings and Speeches That Changed the World*, ed. James Melvin Washington (New York: Harper One, 1992), 104.

[4] Douglas S. Massey, *Categorically Unequal: The American Stratification System* (New York: Russell Sage Foundation, 2007), xvi.

[5] Robert D. Putnam and David E. Campbell, *American Grace: How Religion Divides and Unites Us* (New York: Simon & Schuster, 2010), Kindle Electronic Edition, Location 4427.

[6] King, *I Have a Dream*, 95-98.

[7] Charles Marsh, *The Beloved Community: How Faith Shapes Social Justice, from the Civil Rights Movement to Today* (New York: Basic Books, 2005), 1-2.

[8] All biblical references will be taken from the New International Version, unless otherwise noted.

[9] John W. de Gruchy, *Reconciliation: Restoring Justice* (Minneapolis: Fortress Press, 2002), 34.

[10] Ibid., 19.

[11] Michael Battle, *Reconciliation: The Ubuntu Theology of Desmond Tutu*, rev. ed. (Cleveland: The Pilgrim Press, 2009), 5.

[12] Ibid., 180.

[13] Ibid.

[14] Putnam and Campbell, *American Grace*, Location 588.

[15] de Gruchy, *Reconciliation*, 28.

[16] While avoiding a specific definition of "missional," the authors of *Missional Church* provide this helpful description: "We have arrived at a shared consensus that our definitions of the church should focus on and arise out of the formation of particular communities of God's people, called and sent where they are as witnesses to the gospel." Darrell L. Guder, ed., *Missional Church: A Vision for the Sending of the Church in North America* (Grand Rapids, MI: Wm. B. Eerdmans Publishing Co., 1999), 9.

[17] Massey, *Categorically Unequal*, 52.

## Chapter 1

[18] The Town of Chatham, Virginia, "Visit Chatham," The Town of Chatham, http://chatham-va.gov/visit-chatham (accessed January 27, 2012).

[19] Edward Pearce, *Pitt the Elder: Man of War* (London: The Bodley Head Random House, 2010), Kindle Electronic Edition: Location 6266.

[20] Ibid., Location 6830-6842

[21] The Town of Chatham, Virginia, "Visit Chatham."

[22] Frederick F. Siegel, *The Roots of Southern Distinctiveness: Tobacco and Society in Danville, Virginia, 1780-1865* (Chapel Hill, NC: The University of North Carolina Press, 1987), 27.

[23] Michael Swanson, *Danville, Virginia and the Coming of the Modern South* (Lexington, KY: CreateSpace, 2010), 7.

[24] Larry G. Aaron, *Pittsylvania County Virginia: A Brief History* (Charleston, SC: The History Press, 2009), 122.

[25] "Fire Hoses, Billy Sticks Rout Night Demonstrators," *Danville Register*, June 11, 1963.

Danville, Virginia (WDBJ Television, Roanoke, VA)," University of Virginia, http://www2.vcdh.virginia.edu/civilrightstv/wdbj/segments/WDBJ04_25.html (accessed January 27, 2012).

[27] Siegel, *The Roots of Southern Distinctiveness*, 62.

[28] Ibid., 63.

[29] Ibid.

[30] Aaron, *Pittsylvania County Virginia*, 80.

[31] Ibid., 84.

[32] Kenneth M. Stamp, *The Peculiar Institution: Slavery in the Ante-Bellum South* (1956; reprint, New York: Vintage Books, 1989), 18.

[33] Linda M. Heywood and John K. Thornton, *Central Africans, Atlantic Creoles, and the Foundation of the Americas, 1585-1660* (New York: Cambridge University Press, 2007), 7.

[34] Ibid., 5-6.

[35] Ibid.

[36] Ibid., 8.

[37] Siegel, *The Roots of Southern Distinctiveness*, 17.

[38] Aaron, *Pittsylvania County Virginia*, 87-88.

[39] Ibid., 85.

[40] Siegel, *The Roots of Southern Distinctiveness*, 74.

[41] Robert Sidney Smith, *Mill on the Dan: A History of Dan River Mills, 1882-1950* (Durham, NC: Duke University Press, 1960), 5.

[42] Ibid., 15.

[43] Ibid., 8.

[44] Swanson, *Danville, Virginia and the Coming of the Modern South*, 33-44.

[45] Smith, *Mill on the Dan*, 9.

[46] Ibid.

[47] Ibid., 164.

[48] Ibid., 272.

[49] Ibid., 401.

[50] Smith, *Mill on the Dan*, 509.

[51] Peter Wallenstein, *Cradle of America: Four Centuries of Virginia History* (Lawrence, KS: The University Press of Kansas, 2007), 329.

[52] Ibid., 341.

[53] Matthew D. Lassiter and Andrew B. Lewis, eds. *The Moderates' Dilemma: Massive Resistance to School Desegregation in Virginia* (Charlottesville, VA: University Press of Virginia, 1998), ix-x.

[54] Ibid., 135.

[55] Bob McDonnell, "Meet Bob," Governor Bob McDonnell, http://www.bobmcdonnell.com/meet_bob/ (accessed January 30, 2012).

[56] Anita Kumar and Rosalind S. Helderman, "McDonnell's Confederate History Month proclamation irks civil rights leaders," *The Washington Post*, http://www.washingtonpost.com/wp-dyn/content/article/2010/04/06/AR2010040604416.html (accessed January 28, 2012).

[57] Anita Kumar, "Top McDonnell supporter condemns governor for Confederate History Month," *The Washington Post*, http://voices.washingtonpost.com/virginiapolitics/2010/04/top_mcdonne

ll_ supporter_condem.html (accessed January 28, 2012).

[58] CNN, "Governor McDonnell apologizes for omitting slavery in Confederacy proclamation," CNN.com, http://articles.cnn.com/2010-04-07/politics/virginia.confederate.history_1_slavery-apology-confederate-history-month?_s=PM:POLITICS (accessed January 28, 2012).

[59] Danville Regional Foundation, "Danville-Pittsylvania County, VA Census Briefing," http://drfonline.org/documents/CensusBriefingReport2010.pdf (accessed January 28, 2012).

[60] Ibid.

[61] Danville Regional Foundation, "Danville-Pittsylvania County, VA Census Briefing."

[62] Danville and Pittsylvania County operate separate independent school districts. The Town of Chatham is included in the Pittsylvania County school district.

[63] Danville Regional Foundation, "2010 Regional Report Card," http://drfonline.org/region/ documents/2011/2010-Regional-Report-Card-summary.pdf (accessed January 28, 2012).

[64] Danville Regional Foundation, "Danville-Pittsylvania County, VA Census Briefing."

[65] Jobs for the Future, *Report to the Danville Regional Foundation: Assessment of Workforce Development and Related Educational Challenges and Opportunities* (Boston: Jobs for the Future, 2007), Introduction.

[66] Ibid., 20.

[67] Rich Morin, "Rising Share of Americans See Conflict between Rich and Poor," Pew Research, http://www.pewsocialtrends.org/2012-/01/11/rising-share-of-americans-see-conflict-between-rich-and-poor/ (accessed January 28, 2012).

[68] Sherrow O. Pinder, *Whiteness and Racialized Ethnic Groups in the United States: The Politics of Remembering* (Lanham, MD: Lexington Books, 2012), x.

[69] Jobs for the Future, *Report to the Danville Regional Foundation*, Introduction.

[70] Ibid.

[71] Jobs for the Future, *Report to the Danville Regional Foundation*, 31.

[72] Ibid.

[73] The Virginia Tobacco Indemnification and Community Revitalization Commission, "The Institute for Advanced Learning and Research (IALR)," http://www.tic.virginia.gov/ialr.shtml (accessed January 30, 2012).

[74] Institute for Advanced Learning and Research, "Home," http://ialr.org/ (accessed January 28, 2012).

[75] Danville Regional Foundation, "Vision and Mission," http://drfonline.org/about/vision.php (accessed January 28, 2012).

[76] William A. Blair, *Cities of the Dead: Contesting the Memory of the Civil War in the South, 1865-1914* (Chapel Hill, NC: The University of North Carolina Press, 2004), Kindle Electronic Edition, Location 699.

[77] Mark A. Noll, *The Civil War as a Theological Crisis* (Chapel Hill, NC: The University of North Carolina Press, 2006), Kindle Electronic Edition, Location 438.

[78] Bruce T. Gourley, *Diverging Loyalties: Baptists in Middle Georgia During the Civil War* (Macon, GA: Mercer University Press, 2011), 1.

[79] King, Jr., *I Have a Dream*, 95.

[80] Association of Religion Data Archives, "State Membership Report," http://www.thearda.com/mapsReports/reports/state/51_2000.asp (accessed January 28, 2012).

[81] Association of Religion Data Archives, "County Membership Report, 51590," http://www.thearda.com/mapsReports/reports/counties/51590_2000.asp (accessed January 28, 2012).

[82] Ibid.

[83] Pittsylvania Baptist Association, *2010 Annual of the Pittsylvania Baptist Association* (Danville, VA: Pittsylvania Baptist Association, 2010), 50.

[84] Putnam and Campbell, *American Grace*, Location 4427.

[85] Thriving Rural Communities, "Rev. Chuck Warnock on How a Small Church Has Made a Big Difference," Duke Divinity School, http://divinity.duke.edu/initiatives-centers/thriving-rural-communities/covered-dish/rev-chuck-warnock (accessed January 28, 2012).

[86] Chatham Cares, Inc., "About Us," The Community Center at Chatham, http://chathamcares. org/about-us/ (accessed January 28, 2012).

[87] Chuck Warnock, "Chatham Arts Community Music School," Chuck Warnock Blog, entry posted May 15, 2007, http://chuckwarnockblog.wordpress.com/2007/05/15/chatham-arts-community-music-school/ (accessed January 28, 2012).

## Chapter 2

[88] Bill J. Leonard, *Baptist Ways: A History* (Valley Forge, PA: Judson Press, 2003), 189.

[89] Ella Vaden Aylor, *Centennial of the Chatham Baptist Church: 1857-1957* (Chatham, VA: Star-Tribune, 1957), 2.

[90] Chas. F. Leek, *The History of Pittsylvania Baptist Association: 1788-1963* (Danville, VA: The Pittsylvania Baptist Association, 1963), 95.

[91] Lyle E. Schaller, *Small Congregation, Big Potential: Ministry in the Small Membership Church* (Nashville: Abingdon Press, 2003), 29.

[92] Mark Chaves, *Congregations in America* (Cambridge, MA: Harvard University Press, 2004), 17.

[93] Ibid., 18.

[94] Israel Galindo, *The Hidden Lives of Congregations: Discerning Church Dynamics* (Herndon, VA: The Alban Institute, 2004), 81.

[95] Cynthia Woolever and Deborah Bruce, *A Field Guide to U.S. Congregations: Who's Going Where and Why* (Louisville, KY: Westminster John Knox Press, 2002), 13.

[96] Chaves, *Congregations in America*, 33.

[97] Charles Warnock, "Creating the Future: Leadership and Missional Imagination" (seminar paper, Fuller Theological Seminary, 2006), 50.

[98] Chatham Baptist Church database.

[99] Chaves, *Congregations in America*, 19.

[100] Ibid.

[101] Pittsylvania Baptist Association, *2010 Annual of the Pittsylvania Baptist Association*, 11-15.

[102] Chaves, *Congregations in America*, 127.

[103] Woolever and Bruce, *A Field Guide to U.S. Congregations*, 35.

[104] Charles Warnock, "Appreciative Inquiry Report and Reflection" (seminar paper, Fuller Theological Seminary, 2006), 45.

[105] Page Tredway, *Chatham Baptist Church: A Child's Recollections* (Danville, VA: J. T. Townes Ptg. Co., 1967), 12.

[106] Warnock, "Appreciative Inquiry Report and Reflection," 68.

[107] Galindo, *The Hidden Lives of Congregations*, 73.

[108] Ibid., 72.

[109] Alan J. Roxburgh, *Missional Map-Making: Skills for Leading in Times of Transition* (San Francisco: Jossey-Bass, 2010), 88-89.

[110] Herschel H. Hobbs, *The Baptist Faith and Message*, Rev. ed. (Nashville:

Convention Press, 2004), 64.

[111] Chatham Baptist Church, "Constitution and By-laws" (Chatham, VA: Chatham Baptist Church, 2006), 2.

[112] Chatham Baptist Church, "Policies and Procedures Manual" (Chatham, VA: Chatham Baptist Church, 2006).

[113] Chatham Baptist Church, "Constitution and By-laws," 7.

[114] Woolever and Bruce, *A Field Guide To U.S. Congregations*, 40.

[115] The area typically votes Republican in both federal and state elections, and currently is represented by a Republican United States Representative, a Republican state senator, and a Republican member of the Virginia House of Delegates.

[116] Fisher Humphreys, *The Way We Were: How Southern Baptist Theology Has Changed and What It Means to Us All*, rev. ed. (Macon, GA: Smyth & Helwys Publishing, Inc. 2002), 97-107.

[117] Ibid., 6.

[118] Senior adult member of Chatham Baptist Church, personal interview with the author, 2005.

[119] Chatham Baptist Church, "Constitution and By-laws," 1.

[120] Craig Van Gelder, *The Ministry of the Missional Church: A Community Led by the Spirit* (Grand Rapids, MI: Baker Books, 2007), 18.

[121] Ibid., 41.

[122] Ibid., 44.

[123] Reuben Edward Alley, *A History of Baptists in Virginia* (Richmond, VA: Virginia Baptist General Board, 1973), 278.

[124] Ibid.

[125] Ibid.

[126] Aylor, *Centennial of the Chatham Baptist Church*, 7.

[127] Leek, *The History of The Pittsylvania Baptist Association*, 69.

[128] Wikipedia, "Hargrave Military Academy," http://en.wikipedia.org/wiki/Hargrave_Military_ Academy (accessed February 8, 2012).

[129] Hargrave Military Academy, "Educational Philosophy," http://www.hargrave.edu/admissions/ about-hargrave/educational-philosophy/ (accessed February 13, 2012).

[130] The Southern Baptist Convention's "30,000 Movement" had a goal of establishing ten thousand churches and twenty thousand missions between 1956 and 1965. See Baptist Press, "Press Release: September 3, 1960," Southern Baptist History Library and Archives http://media.sbhla.org.s3.amazonaws. com/1093,03-Sep-1960.pdf (accessed February 10, 2012).

[131] Leek, *The History of The Pittsylvania Baptist Association*, 163.

[132] Pittsylvania Baptist Association, *2010 Annual of the Pittsylvania Baptist Association*, 50.

[133] Chuck Warnock, "Learn to Partner: How One Church, Working with Community Groups, Is Making a Big Difference in a Small Town," *Leadership* (Spring 2007): 109-10.

[134] The Boys and Girls Club of the Danville Area, "Locations and Directions," http://www.bgcdanville.org/index.php?option=com_content&view=article&id =109&Itemid=183 (accessed February 13, 2012).

[135] Warnock, "Learn To Partner," 109-11.

[136] Ray Oldenburg, *The Great Good Place: Cafes, Coffee Shops, Bookstores, Bars, Hair Salons, and Other Hangouts at the Heart of a Community* (New York: Marlowe & Company, 1999), xvii.

[137] The Community Center at Chatham, "Building Use," Chatham Cares, Inc., http://chathamcares. org/building-use/ (accessed February 13, 2012).

[138] Chatham Baptist Church, "1969 Handbook" (Chatham, VA: Chatham Baptist Church).

[139] Warnock, "Creating the Future," 13.

[140] Warnock, "Appreciative Inquiry Report and Reflection," 45.

[141] Ibid., 46.

## Chapter 3

[142] James Wm. McClendon, *Doctrine: Systematic Theology, Volume II* (Nashville: Abingdon Press, 1994), Preface.

[143] Ibid.

[144] Ibid.

[145] James Wm. McClendon, *Ethics: Systematic Theology, Volume I*, Revised Edition (Nashville: Abingdon Press, 2002), 32.

[146] McClendon quotes the Scripture using the King James Version. Italics are McClendon's.

[147] McClendon, *Ethics*, 32-33. McClendon contends that "all parts (and all volumes) of the system presuppose one another" (McClendon, *Doctrine*, 327). This ministry focus paper includes references from McClendon's *Ethics: Volume I* as a result of McClendon's approach.

[148] Ibid.

[149] McClendon, *Doctrine*, 395.

[150] McClendon, *Ethics*, 32.

[151] McClendon, *Doctrine*, 343.

[152] Ibid.

[153] Ibid., 327.

[154] Ibid., 332.

[155] Ibid., 343.

[156] Ibid.

[157] Ibid., 364.

[158] John Howard Yoder, *Body Politics: Five Practices of the Christian Community before the Watching World* (Scottdale, PA: Herald Press, 1992), ix.

[159] Ibid., x.

[160] Ibid., vii.

[161] Ibid., 7.

[162] Ibid., 3.

[163] Ibid., 7-8.

[164] Ibid., 21-22.

[165] Ibid., 33.

[166] Ibid.

[167] Ibid., 34.

[168] Ibid., 47.

[169] Ibid., 60.

[170] Ibid.

[171] Ibid., 61.

[172] Ibid., 70.

[173] Ibid., 67.

[174] David W. Augsburger, *Helping People Forgive* (Louisville, KY: Westminster John Knox Press, 1996), x.

[175] Ibid., 147.

[176] Ibid., ix.

[177] Ibid., 6.

[178] Ibid., 9.

[179] Ibid.

[180] Ibid., 11.

[181] Ibid., 23.

[182] Ibid., 31.

[183] Ibid., 53.

[184] Ibid., 74.

[185] Ibid., 104.

[186] Ibid., 112.

[187] Ibid., 145.

[188] Ibid., 149.

[189] Ibid., 163.

[190] Ibid., 164.

[191] John Paul Lederach, *The Moral Imagination: The Art and Soul of Building Peace* (New York: Oxford University Press, 2005), vii.

[192] Ibid., ix.

[193] University of Notre Dame, "Curriculum Vitae of John Paul Lederach," http://kroc.nd.edu/ sites/default/files/lederachcv.pdf (accessed September 8, 2012).

[194] Lederach, *The Moral Imagination*, ix.

[195] Ibid., 5.

[196] Ibid., ix.

[197] Ibid., vii.

[198] Ibid., x.

[199] Ibid., 7-10.

[200] Ibid., 10-13.

[201] Ibid., 13-16.

[202] Ibid., 16-19.

[203] Ibid., 19.

[204] Ibid., 28 and 52.

[205] Ibid., 164.

[206] Ibid., x.

[207] L. Gregory Jones, *Embodying Forgiveness: A Theological Analysis* (Grand Rapids, MI: Wm. B. Eerdmans Publishing Co., 1995), xii.

[208] Ibid.

[209] Ibid.

[210] Ibid.

[211] Ibid., xiii.

[212] Ibid., 50.

[213] Ibid., 49.

[214] Ibid., 113.

[215] Ibid., 111.

[216] Ibid., 131.

[217] Ibid., 166-85.

[218] Ibid., 207.

[219] Ibid., 231-32.

[220] Ibid., 232.

[221] Bryant L. Myers, *Walking with the Poor: Principles and Practices of Transformational Development* (Maryknoll, NY: Orbis Books, 2011), 1.

[222] Ibid., 3.

[223] Ibid., 10.

[224] Ibid., 12.

[225] Ibid., 50.

[226] Ibid., 51.

[227] Ibid.

[228] Ibid., 65.

[229] Ibid., 67.

[230] Ibid., 115-20.

[231] Ibid., 151.

[232] Ibid., 152.

[233] Ani Kalayjian and Raymond F. Paloutzian, eds., *Forgiveness and Reconciliation: Psychological Pathways to Conflict Transformation and Peace Building* (New York: Springer, 2009), vii.

[234] Ibid., 3-79.

[235] Ibid., 83-151.

[236] Ibid., 155-282.

[237] Ibid., vii

[238] Ibid., 55.

[239] Ibid., 69.

## Chapter 4

[240] Veli-Matti Karkkainen, *Introduction to Ecclesiology: Ecumenical, Historical and Global Perspectives* (Downers Grove, IL: InterVarsity Press, 2002), 9.

[241] McClendon, *Systematic Theology: Ethics: Volume 1*, 21.

[242] Walter B. Shurden, *The Baptist Identity: Four Fragile Freedoms* (Macon, GA: Smyth and Helwys Publishing, Inc., 1993), 4-6.

[243] Ibid., 23.

[244] E. Y. Mullins, *The Axioms of Religion*, ed. C. Douglas Weaver (Macon, GA: Mercer University Press, 2010), 66.

[245] Ibid., 259.

[246] Shurden, *The Baptist Identity*, 24.

[247] David W. Bebbington, *Baptists through the Centuries: A History of a Global People* (Waco, TX: Baylor University Press, 2012), 259.

[248] Humphreys, *The Way We Were*, 36.

[249] Ibid., 39-40.

[250] Shurden, *The Baptist Identity*, 10-21.

[251] Hobbs, *The Baptist Faith and Message*, rev. ed., 94.

[252] Humphreys, *The Way We Were*, 40.

[253] Shurden, *The Baptist Identity*, 31.

[254] Ibid., 33.

[255] Hobbs, *The Baptist Faith and Message*, vi.

[256] Ibid., 64.

[257] Ibid., 65.

[258] Michael E. Williams, Sr. and Walter B. Shurden, eds., *Turning Points in Baptist History: A Festschrift in Honor of Harry Leon McBeth* (Macon, GA: Mercer University Press, 2008), 63.

[259] McClendon, Jr., *Systematic Theology: Doctrine: Volume II*, 334.

[260] Shurden, *The Baptist Identity*, 9.

[261] Hobbs, *The Baptist Faith and Message*, 19.

[262] Southern Baptist Convention, "Comparison of the 1925, 1963 and 2000 Baptist Faith and Message," http://sbc.org/bfm/bfmcomparison.asp (accessed September 27, 2012).

[263] Shurden, *The Baptist Identity*, 10.

[264] Ibid., 12.

[265] Ibid., 18-19.

[266] Hobbs, *The Baptist Faith and Message*, 121.

[267] Shurden, *The Baptist Identity*, 45.

[268] Bebbington, *Baptists through the Centuries*, 197.

[269] William R. Estep, *The Anabaptist Story: An Introduction to Sixteenth-Century Anabaptism*, 3rd ed. (Grand Rapids, MI: William B. Eerdmans Publishing Company, 1996), 257.

[270] Leonard, *Baptist Ways*, 130-31.

[271] Hobbs, *The Baptist Faith and Message*, 64.

[272] Shurden, *The Baptist Identity*, 5-6.

[273] Ibid., 6.

[274] William R. Estep, *Whole Gospel, Whole World: The Foreign Mission Board of the Southern Baptist Convention 1845-1995* (Nashville: Broadman & Holman Publishers, 1994), 5.

[275] Ibid., 49.

[276] David Roach, "WRIGHT: Keep Legal Name; Add Informal Descriptor 'Great Commission Baptists,'" *SBC Life: Journal of the Southern Baptist Convention*, http://www.sbclife.net/Articles/ 2012/03/Sla1.asp (accessed September 27, 2012).

[277] Mullins, *The Axioms of Religion*, 9.

[278] Ibid., 10-11.

[279] Ibid., 22.

[280] Harold Bloom, *The American Religion*, 2d ed. (New York: Chu Hartley Publishers, 2006), 220.

[281] McClendon, *Ethics*, 29.

[282] Shurden, *The Baptist Identity*, 33.

[283] Baptist Press, "SBC severs ties with BWA as theological concerns remain," http://www.bpnews. net/bpnews.asp?id=18475 (accessed September 27, 2012).

[284] James William McClendon, "What Is Southern Baptist Ecumenism?" *Southwestern Journal of Theology* 10 (Spring 1968): 73.

[285] Shurden, *The Baptist Identity*, 90.

[286] Williams, *Turning Points in Baptist History*, 269-70.

[287] Leonard, *Baptist in America*, 130.

[288] Humphreys, *The Way We Were*, 112.

[289] Leonard, *Baptists in America*, 130.

[290] Ibid., 142.

[291] Bloom, *The American Religion*, 221.

[292] Ibid., 238.

[293] The grammatically incorrect phrase "me and Jesus" comes from a Country Gospel song written by Tom T. Hall, titled "Me and Jesus." Country Music Hall of Fame and Museum, "Tom T. Hall," http://countrymusichalloffame.org/full-list-of-inductees/view/tom-t-hall (accessed September 27, 2012).

[294] David Augsburger, *Dissident Discipleship: A Spirituality of Self-Surrender, Love of God, and Love of Neighbor* (Grand Rapids, MI: Brazos Press, 2006), 12.

[295] James Leo Garrett, *Baptist Theology: A Four-Century Study* (Macon, GA: Mercer University Press, 2009), 539.

[296] Gary A. Furr and Curtis W. Freeman, *Ties That Bind: Life Together in the Baptist Vision* (Macon, GA: Smyth and Helwys Publishing, Inc., 1994), 41.

[297] Williams, *Turning Points in Baptist History*, 176-77.

[298] United States Government Archives, "The Bill of Rights," http://www.archives.gov /exhibits/charters/bill_of_rights_transcript.html (accessed October 6, 2012).

[299] Shurden, *The Baptist Identity*, 51.

[300] Ibid., 53.

[301] Ibid., 52-53.

[302] C. Norman Kraus, ed., *Evangelicalism and Anabaptism* (Eugene, OR: Wipf and Stock Publishers, 1979), 40.

[303] Ibid., 180.

[304] Mark A. Noll, *American Evangelical Christianity: An Introduction* (Malden, MA: Blackwell Publishers Inc., 2001), 188-89.

[305] Humphreys, *The Way We Were*, 130.

[306] William Brackney, as quoted in Leonard, *Baptists in America*, 181.

[307] Ibid.

[308] Guder, ed., *Missional Church*, 6.

[309] Ibid.

[310] Alan J. Roxburgh and M. Scott Boren, *Introducing the Missional Church: What It Is, Why It Matters, How to Become One* (Grand Rapids, MI: Baker Books, 2009), 101-02.

[311] Harold S. Bender, *The Anabaptist Vision* (Scottsdale, PA: Herald Press, 1944), 20.

[312] Ibid., 20-21.

[313] C. Norman Kraus, *The Community of the Spirit: How the Church Is in the World* (Eugene, OR: Wipf and Stock Publishers, 1993), 35.

[314] Ibid., 39.

[315] Ibid., 50.

[316] Ibid., 53.

[317] Ibid.

[318] Augsburger, *Dissident Discipleship*, 14-15.

[319] Alan Kreider, Eleanor Kreider, and Paulus Widjaja, *A Culture of Peace: God's Vision for the Church* (Intercourse, PA: Good Books, 2005), 99.

[320] John Howard Yoder, *The Priestly Kingdom: Social Ethics as Gospel* (University of Notre Dame, 1984), 43.

[321] Kreider, Kreider, and Widjaja, *A Culture of Peace*, 99.

[322] Ibid.

[323] Ibid., 102.

[324] Ibid., 106.

[325] Ibid., 108.

[326] Ibid., 109.

[327] Ibid.

[328] Ted Grimsrud, *Embodying the Way of Jesus: Anabaptist Convictions for the Twenty-First Century* (Eugene, OR: Wipf and Stock Publishers, 2007), 112.

[329] Kraus, *Evangelicalism and Anabaptism*, 179-80.

[330] Grimsrud, *Embodying the Way of Jesus*, 58-59.

[331] Ibid., 120.

[332] Bender, *The Anabaptist Vision*, 3.

[333] Ibid., 20.

[334] Ibid., 26.

[335] Ibid., 31.

[336] John D. Roth, ed., *Engaging Anabaptism: Conversations with a Radical Tradition* (Scottdale, PA: Herald Press, 2001), 24.

[337] Augsburger, *Dissident Discipleship*, 74.

[338] Grimsrud, *Embodying the Way of Jesus*, 123.

[339] Kreider, Kreider, and Widjaja, *A Culture of Peace*, 16-17.

[340] John Howard Yoder, *He Came Preaching Peace* (Scottdale, PA: Herald Press, 2004), 24.

[341] Perry B. Yoder and Willard M. Swartley, eds., *The Meaning of Peace: Biblical Studies* (Elkhart, IN: Institute of Mennonite Studies, 2001), 25.

[342] Perry B. Yoder, *Shalom: The Bible's Word for Salvation, Justice, and Peace* (Nappanee, IN: Evangel Publishing House, 1987), 21.

[343] Kreider, Kreider, and Widjaja, *A Culture of Peace*, 14.

[344] Hobbs, *The Baptist Faith and Message*, 19.

## Chapter 5

[345] Gregory Baum and Howard Wells, eds., *The Reconciliation of Peoples: Challenge to the Churches* (Eugene, OR: Wipf and Stock Publishers, 2009), 3.

[346] George Arthur Buttrick, ed., *The Interpreter's Dictionary of the Bible: An Illustrated Encyclopedia, Volume 4* (Nashville: Abingdon Press, 1962), 16.

[347] Ibid., 16.

[348] Walter Brueggemann, ed. Patrick D. Miller, *Deep Memory, Exuberant Hope: Contested Truth in a Post-Christian World* (Minneapolis: Fortress Press, 2000), 61.

[349] Ibid., 68.

[350] Ibid., 60.

[351] Ibid.

[352] Ibid., 68.

[353] Yoder, *Body Politics*, 1.

[354] Glenn H. Stassen and David P. Gushee, *Kingdom Ethics: Following Jesus in Contemporary Context* (Downers Grove, IL: InterVarsity Press, 203), 51.

[355] Richard B. Hays, *The Moral Vision of the New Testament: Community, Cross,*

*New Creation: A Contemporary Introduction to New Testament Ethics* (New York: HarperCollins Publishers, 1996), 103.

356 Augsburger, *Helping People Forgive*, 37.

357 Ibid., 40, 65.

358 Ibid., 40.

359 The Southern Baptist Convention, "Resolution on Racial Reconciliation on the 150th Anniversary of the Southern Baptist Convention," http://www.sbc.net/resolutions/amresolution.asp?id=899 (accessed October 26, 2012).

360 Augsburger, *Helping People Forgive*, 43.

361 David Augsburger, *The New Freedom of Forgiveness*, 3rd ed. (Chicago: Moody Publishers, 2000), 32.

362 Augsburger, *Helping People Forgive*, 11.

363 Jones, *Embodying Forgiveness*, xii.

364 Ibid.

365 Ibid., 16.

366 Ray Anderson, *The Shape of Practical Theology: Empowering Ministry with Theological Praxis* (Downers Grove, IL: InterVarsity Press, 2001), 296-98.

367 David W. Augsburger, *Conflict Mediation across Cultures: Pathways and Patterns* (Louisville, KY: Westminster John Knox Press, 1992), 281.

368 Margaret Urban Walker, *Moral Repair: Reconstructing Moral Relations after Wrongdoing* (New York: Cambridge University Press, 2006), 191.

369 Elie Wiesel, *Night*, trans. Marion Wiesel (New York: Hill and Wang, 2006), xv.

370 Jarem Sawatsky, *Justpeace Ethics: A Guide to Restorative Justice and Peacebuilding* (Eugene, OR: Cascade Books, 2008), 77.

[371] Brian Cox, *Faith-Based Reconciliation: A Moral Vision That Transforms People and Societies* (Lexington, KY: Xlibris Corporation, 2007), 87.

[372] Desmond Mpilo Tutu, *No Future without Forgiveness* (New York: Doubleday, 1999), Kindle Electronic Edition, location 367.

[373] Glenn H. Stassen, ed., *Just Peacemaking: The New Paradigm for the Ethics of Peace and War* (Cleveland, OH: The Pilgrim Press, 2008), 101.

[374] A superordinate goal has been defined as a goal "that cannot be easily ignored by members of the two antagonistic groups, but whose attainment is beyond the resources and efforts of one group alone." Muzafer Sherif, O. J. Harvey, B. Jack White, William R. Hood, and Carolyn W. Shief, *The Robbers Cave Experiment: Intergroup Conflict and Cooperation* (Middleton, CT: Wesleyan University Press, 1988), 23.

[375] de Gruchy, *Reconciliation: Restoring Justice*, 15.

[376] Lassiter and Lewis, *The Moderates' Dilemma*, 20.

[377] Erin Daly and Jeremy Sarkin, *Reconciliation in Divided Societies: Finding Common Ground* (Philadelphia: University of Pennsylvania Press, 2007), 5.

[378] Ibid., 12.

[379] Mark A. Noll, *God and Race in American Politics: A Short History* (Princeton University Press, 2008), 176.

[380] Miguel A. De La Torre, *Liberating Jonah: Forming an Ethics of Reconciliation* (Maryknoll, NY: Orbis Books, 2007), 90.

[381] Pinder, *Whiteness and Racialized Ethnic Groups in the United States*, x.

[382] Lederach, *The Moral Imagination*, 9.

[383] James C. Livingston, *Anatomy of the Sacred: An Introduction to Religion*, 6th ed. (Upper Saddle River, NJ: Pearson Prentice Hall, 2009), 345.

[384] Harold Coward and Gordon S. Smith, eds., *Religion and Peacebuilding* (Albany, NY: State University of New York Press, 2004), 2.

[385] Daly and Sarkin, *Reconciliation in Divided Societies*, 11-12.

[386] Robert D. Enright and Richard P. Fitzgibbons, *Helping Clients Forgive: An Empirical Guide for Resolving Anger and Restoring Hope* (Washington, D. C.: American Psychological Association, 2000), 24.

[387] Ibid., 18-19.

[388] Everett L. Worthington, Jr., *Dimensions of Forgiveness: Psychological Research and Theological Perspectives* (Radnor, PA: Templeton Foundation Press, 1998), 113-28.

[389] Enright and Fitzgibbons, *Helping Clients Forgive*, 24-25.

[390] Ibid., xi.

[391] Vincent N. Parillo, *Understanding Race and Ethnic Relations*, 4th ed. (Boston: Allyn & Bacon, 2012), 17.

[392] Ibid., 19.

[393] Massey, *Categorically Unequal*, 1.

[394] Eduardo Bonilla-Silva, *Racism without Racists: Color-Blind Racism and the Persistence of Racial Inequality in the United States*, 3rd ed. (Lanham, MD: Rowman and Littlefied Publishers, Inc., 2010), 8.

[395] Ibid., 3.

[396] John Paul Lederach, *Building Peace: Sustainable Reconciliation in Divided Societies* (Washington, D. C.: United States Institute of Peace Press, 1997), 29.

[397] Ibid., 31.

[398] Ibid.

[399] Ibid.

[400] Kraus, *The Community of the Spirit*, 9.

[401] Ibid., 14.

[402] Ibid., 116.

[403] Ibid., 52.

[404] Ibid., 55.

[405] Ibid., 56.

[406] Ibid., 59.

[407] Ibid., 63.

[408] Ibid.

[409] William Klassen, *The Forgiving Community* (Philadelphia: The Westminster Press, 1966), 143.

[410] Glen Harold Stassen, *A Thicker Jesus: Incarnational Discipleship in a Secular Age* (Louisville, KY: Westminster John Knox Press, 2012), Kindle Edition, Location 774.

[411] Augsburger, *Helping People Forgive*, 116.

[412] Ibid., 117.

[413] Ibid., 156.

[414] Robert J. Schreiter, *Reconciliation: Mission and Ministry in a Changing Social Order*, The Boston Theological Institute Series, Volume 3 (Maryknoll, NY: Orbis Books and Newton, MA: Boston Theological Institute, 1992), 71-72.

[415] Ibid., 72-73.

[416] Ibid., 73.

[417] Ibid.

[418] Ibid.

[419] Bruce C. Birch, Walter Brueggemann, Terence E. Fretheim, and David

L. Petersen, *A Theological Introduction to the Old Testament*, 2nd ed. (Nashville: Abingdon Press, 2005), 155.

[420] Ibid.

[421] Ibid.

[422] N. T. Wright, *The New Testament and the People of God* (Minneapolis: Fortress Press, 1992), 362-63.

[423] Ibid., 363.

[424] William A. Clebsch and Charles R. Jaeckle, *Pastoral Care in Historical Perspective* (Englewood, NJ: Prentice-Hall, 1964), 34-66, as quoted in William H. Willimon, *Worship as Pastoral Care* (Nashville: Abingdon Press, 1979), 31.

[425] William H. Willimon, *Worship as Pastoral Care* (Nashville: Abingdon Press, 1979), 32.

[426] Ibid., 33.

[427] Ibid., 35.

[428] Dietrich Bonhoeffer, *Dietrich Bonhoeffer Works, Volume I, Sanctorum Communio*, trans. Reinhard Krauss and Nancy Lukens, ed. Clifford J. Green (Minneapolis: Fortress Press, 1998), 230.

[429] Ibid., 231.

[430] Ibid., 228-29.

[431] Ibid., 229.

## Chapter 6

[432] Yoder, *He Came Preaching Peace*, 116.

[433] Walter Brueggemann, *Peace* (St. Louis, MO: Chalice Press, 2001), 14.

[434] Ibid.

[435] Ibid., 15.

[436] Ibid.

[437] David J. Bosch, *Transforming Mission: Paradigm Shifts in Theology of Mission* (Maryknoll, NY: Orbis Books, 2007), 119.

[438] Ibid.

[439] Ibid., 116.

[440] Ibid.

[441] Ibid.

[442] Ibid.

[443] Yoder, *He Came Preaching Peace*, 122.

[444] Ibid.

[445] Ibid.

[446] Roxburgh and Boren, *Introducing the Missional Church*, 45.

[447] Ibid., 42.

[448] Ibid.

[449] Ibid.

[450] Ibid., 43.

[451] Ibid., 44.

[452] Ibid., 45.

[453] Yoder, *Body Politics*, ix.

[454] Roxburgh and Boren, *Introducing the Missional Church*, 71.

[455] Ibid.

[456] Mark DeYmaz, *Building a Healthy Multi-Ethnic Church: Mandate, Commitments, and Practices of a Diverse Congregation* (San Francisco: Jossey-Bass, 2007), xxvii.

[457] Ibid.

[458] Ibid.

[459] Putnam and Campbell, *American Grace*, Location 4427.

[460] Michael O. Emerson and Rodney M. Woo, *People of the Dream: Multiracial Congregations in the United States* (Princeton University Press, 2006), 173.

[461] Ibid., 192.

[462] David L. Cooperrider and Diana Whitney, *Appreciative Inquiry: A Positive Revolution in Change* (San Francisco: Berrett-Koehler Publishers, Inc., 2005), 8.

[463] Dennis Okholm, ed., *The Gospel in Black and White: Theological Resources for Racial Reconciliation* (Downers Grove, IL: InterVarsity Press, 1997), 149.

[464] Soong-Chan Rah, *The Next Evangelicalism: Freeing the Church from Western Cultural Captivity* (Downers Grove, IL: InterVarsity Press, 2009), 203.

[465] Emerson and Woo, *People of the Dream*, 145.

[466] Rah, *The Next Evangelicalism*, 201.

[467] Ibid., 148.

[468] Emerson and Woo, *People of the Dream*, 155.

[469] Rah, *The Next Evangelicalism*, 205.

[470] Bonilla-Silva, *Racism without Racists*, 8.

[471] Ibid., 9.

[472] Bob Allen, "Southern Baptists elect black president," Associated Baptist Press, http://abpnews.com/ministry/organizations/item/7540-southern-

baptists-elect-black-president#. UQRZBkqjeOE (accessed January 26, 2013).

[473] Wm. Dwight McKissic, Sr., "Lessons from the Animal Kingdom," weblog entry dated March 12, 2011, http://dwightmckissic.wordpress.com/2011/03/12/lessons-from-the-animal-kingdom (accessed January 26, 2013).

[474] Bosch, *Transforming Mission*, 390.

[475] Lois Barrett, "Missional Witness: The Church as Apostle to the World," in Guder, *Missional Church*, 110.

[476] Ibid., 114.

[477] Ibid., 117.

[478] Ibid.

[479] Ibid., 120-22.

[480] Ibid.

[481] Ibid., 128-32.

[482] Ibid., 133-36.

[483] Ibid.

[484] Lederach, *The Moral Imagination*, ix.

[485] Barbara Braver, ed., *I Have Called You Friends: Reflections on Reconciliation: In Honor of Frank T. Griswold* (Cambridge, MA: Cowley Publications, 2006), 4-5.

[486] Ibid.

[487] Ibid.

[488] Ibid., 5-6.

[489] Enright and Fitzgibbons, *Helping Clients Forgive*, 18-19.

[490] Ibid.

[491] Ibid., 30-31.

[492] Augsburger, *Helping People Forgive*, 156.

[493] Ibid.

[494] Ibid., 157.

[495] Ibid., 158-59.

[496] Myers, *Walking with the Poor*, 184.

[497] Emmanuel Kantongole and Chris Rice, *Reconciling All Things: A Christian Vision for Justice, Peace and Healing* (Downers Grove, IL; InterVarsity Press, 2008), Kindle Electronic Edition, Location 19.

[498] Martin Doblmeier, Dan Juday, and Adele Schmidt, *The Power of Forgiveness*, DVD, 2007.

## Chapter 7

[499] Kay Pranis, *The Litte Book of Circle Processes: A New/Old Approach to Peacemaking* (Intercourse, PA: Good Books, 2005), 11.

[500] Ibid., 7-10.

[501] Ibid., 8.

## Summary and Conclusion

[502] David E. Fitch, *The End of Evangelicalism? Discerning a New Faithfulness for Mission: Towards an Evangelical Political Theology* (Eugene, OR: Cascade Books, 2011), Kindle Electronic Edition, Location 371-382.

[503] Ibid., Location 3516-3523.

[504] Ibid., Location 6591.

[505] Ibid., Location 194.

[506] Ibid., Location 211.

[507] Ibid., Location 218.

[508] Ibid., Location 3502.

[509] Ibid.

[510] Ibid., Location 3556.

[511] Ibid., Location 3563.

[512] Ibid., Location 3570.

[513] Ibid., Location 3586.

[514] Ibid., Location 4267.

[515] Ibid., Location 4396.

[516] Marsh, *The Beloved Community*, 1-2.

Made in the USA
Columbia, SC
21 April 2018